V13

V13

CHRONICLE
of a
TRIAL

EMMANUEL CARRÈRE

Translated from the French by John Lambert

Postscript by Grégoire Leménager

Farrar, Straus and Giroux
New York

Farrar, Straus and Giroux
120 Broadway, New York 10271

Library of Congress Cataloging-in-Publication Data
Names: Carrère, Emmanuel, 1957– author. | Lambert, John, 1960– translator. |
Leménager, Grégoire, writer of postscript.
Title: V13 : chronicle of a trial / Emmanuel Carrère ; translated from the French
by John Lambert ; postscript by Grégoire Leménager.
Other titles: V13. English
Description: First American edition. | New York : Farrar, Straus and Giroux, 2024.
Identifiers: LCCN 2024017467 | ISBN 9780374615703 (hardcover)
Subjects: LCSH: Trials (Terrorism)—France—Paris—History—21st century. |
Trials (Blasphemy)—France—Paris—History—21st century. | Terrorism—
Law and legislation—France—Paris—History—21st century. | Charlie
Hebdo Attack, Paris, France, 2015 | Charlie hebdo. | Freedom of expression—
France—History—21st century. | Freedom of the press—France—History—
21st century. | Terrorism—Religious aspects—Islam. | Blasphemy (Islam)—
History—21st century.
Classification: LCC KJV131.C43 C3513 2024 | DDC 345.44/02317—
dc23/eng/20240512
LC record available at https://lccn.loc.gov/2024017467

Contents

The Victims

The Accused

CONTENTS

The Court

CONTENTS

The Victims

Day one

Getting started

Noon, 8 September 2021. Central Paris, Île de la Cité, under a heavy police guard. For the first time, several hundred of us walk through the security gates which we'll pass through every day for the next year. Chances are we'll often say hello to the gendarmes we now greet. Soon we'll be all too familiar with these lawyers with badges hanging from black cords around their necks, these journalists with orange cords, these victims with green or red cords. Some will become friends: the small group of people with whom we'll make the crossing, exchanging notes and impressions, sitting in for each other when the day grows too long, going out for late-night drinks at the brasserie Les Deux Palais when it all becomes too much. The questions on all of our lips: Will you come to all the sessions? Often at least? How will you organise your time? What about your family? Your children? Some, it's clear, will only come on the days expected to be the most intense. Others have vowed to come to every session, the slow days as well as the highlights. I'm one of them. Will I hold out?

The schedule

At the end of July we learned that the trial wouldn't last six months, but nine. A school year, a pregnancy. The programme itself hadn't changed. What had was the time allotted to the plaintiffs. There are around 1,800 of them, and it's still not known how many will testify. They'll be able to add or remove their names until the last minute. Each will be given half an hour on average – but who's going to say 'time's up' to someone who's searching for words to describe the hell of the Bataclan? The half-hour could become an hour, the six months are looking more like a year, and I cannot be the only one today wondering why I'm getting ready to spend a year of my life shut away in a giant courtroom wearing a face mask, waking up at dawn five days a week to type up my notes from the previous day before they become illegible – all of which clearly means thinking of nothing else and having no life for a year. Why? Why inflict this on myself? Why did I offer to write this series of articles for the weekly *L'Obs*? If I were a lawyer or any other player in the grand judicial apparatus, of course I'd do my bit. Ditto if I were a journalist. But a writer whom no one has asked to do this, and who, as the Lacanian psychoanalysts say, is only authorised by his desire? A strange desire, this one. Neither I nor anyone I knew was affected by the attacks. On the other hand, I am interested in justice. In one of my books, *The Adversary*, I describe the grand proceedings of a criminal court; in another, *Other Lives But Mine*, the obscure work of a city court. The trial that gets under way today will not be the Nuremberg of terrorism, as some have said: whereas high Nazi dignitaries were put on trial in Nuremberg, here the defendants are second stringers, since those who did the killing are dead. Nevertheless this trial too will be enormous, unprecedented, something I want to witness: that's one reason. Another is that, without being a specialist in Islam – let alone in Arab studies – I am interested in religions, their pathological mutations, and the question: where does this pathology begin? When it comes to God, where does the madness start? What goes on in these guys' minds? But the main reason is that hundreds of human beings who share the experience of having lived through the night of 13 November 2015, who survived it or survived their loved ones, will stand before us and speak. Day in, day out, we will hear extreme experiences of death and life, and I think that between the time we first enter this courtroom and when we leave it for good, something in all of us will have shifted ground. We don't know what we're waiting for; we don't know what will happen. We go in.

The white box

It's often been said that this would be the trial of the century, a trial for history, an exemplary trial. Many wondered what setting would be worthy of this giant ad for the judicial system. The new courthouse which opened three years ago at the Porte de Clichy in the north of Paris? Too modern, too out of the way. Some gymnasium? Not dignified enough. An auditorium? In bad taste, after the Bataclan. Finally the decision was taken to hold it in the venerable Palais de Justice on the Île de la Cité, between the Sainte-Chapelle built by St Louis in the thirteenth century and the Quai des Orfèvres, where the shadow of Simenon's Inspector Maigret still lurks. And since none of its rooms was big enough, this windowless, 7,000-square-foot white plywood room costing the state 7 million euros and holding up to six hundred people was built in the front lobby. Even at that there isn't enough room for everyone to enter on this first day, so we journalists draw lots to see who can go in. There are three of us from *L'Obs* alone: Violette Lazard and Mathieu Delahousse – who will cover the trial for the website at the feverish pace of one column per day – and me, following events for the magazine at the comfortable rate of 1,400 words per week, handed in on Monday, published on Thursday, the old-fashioned way. We hope our accounts will complement each other. Violette and Mathieu are big names in the legal press – a warm, closely knit guild rich in strong personalities, with whom I've worked a bit in the past and whom I'm happy to rub shoulders with again. I find their company reassuring, and, good comrades that they are, they welcome the novice who's been allowed to string along. *L'Obs* is allotted one seat, they insist I should take it as a welcoming gift. I find myself squeezed in between the special correspondents from the *New York Times* and *Radio Classique*. Even this venerable classical music station has sent someone, it's nuts, but Violette and Mathieu reassure me: soon things will calm down. The TV crews who're now pacing back and forth at the entrance to the courtroom – it's forbidden to film inside – will soon pack up and leave, the correspondent from *Radio Classique* will go back to his symphonies, and only the pros will be left, the specialists in crime and terrorism. Inside the courtroom the benches are extremely uncomfortable: angular, without even the thinnest covering. No desk or tablet arm: whether you write directly on the computer or, like me, in a notebook, you can't help thinking that month after month of taking notes on your knees, constantly changing position to keep the pain to a minimum, will be gruelling. And what's more we're far from the goings-on at the front of the courtroom, so far that we'll spend most of our time following on the big screens overhead. In fact it's a bit like watching the whole thing on television. At 12.25 p.m. a tremor runs through the hall. Heavily escorted by gendarmes, the accused enter the bulletproof box. Most of what we see is the reflection in the glass, and not the defendants behind it. We stand up, crane our necks, and wonder: is he there? Yes, he is. Salah Abdeslam is there. He's the one in the black polo shirt, the furthest from us, the only surviving member of the commando. If he's at the back of the box it's not to prevent us from seeing him but because they're seated in alphabetical order. He's the first in a long series of A's: Abdeslam, Abrini, Amri, Attou, Ayari. A bell rings shrilly and a voice says: 'All rise.' Everyone stands, as if at Mass. The presiding judge and the four assistant judges come in and take their seats. With a hint of a Marseille accent, the presiding judge says: 'Please be seated, the court is now in session.' It's begun.

In the glass box

The roll call

In French criminal cases justice is dispensed by a jury composed of citizens who are selected by drawing lots. For fear of reprisals, in terrorism cases the court is composed of judges for whom such risks are part of the job. Here in addition to the presiding judge there are four other judges – to be precise, four women judges. You get used to it, but the effect is somewhat bizarre and has to do with the fact that the French judiciary is both macho and predominantly female – which in turn has to do with the fact that it's increasingly poorly paid. It's often said that the *Charlie Hebdo* trial which took place last January ran into trouble because the presiding judge lacked authority, and that for this reason the choice now fell on Jean-Louis Périès, a shrewd, solid judge who's close to retirement. His grandfather was a clerk at the district court in Foix on the Spanish border, his father the examining magistrate in the Dominici affair – the rural tragedy that took the nation by storm in the 1950s. Judge Périès too has a country air to him. Or the air of a teacher of the old school, severe at first glance but with a good heart. The first thing he does is call the roll. Fourteen of the twenty defendants on trial are present, and eleven of those present are in the box. That may seem complicated, but as I've spent the summer going over a 378-page document called the OMA – the *ordonnance de mise en accusation* or order of indictment – I can follow along. The OMA summarises in its 378 pages a legal brief comprising 542 volumes which, they say, would be fifty-three metres high if stacked one on top of the other. The nine members of the commando that killed 130 people at the Stade de France, the Bataclan and on the café terraces in eastern Paris are all dead. Judicial action is terminated in their regard. Six others failed to respond to the court summons 'without a valid excuse', Judge Périès says sternly (in fact they do have one, namely that they're also dead, but since no one can be one hundred per cent sure they still stand accused). Of the remaining fourteen, three are not currently under arrest and appear as free individuals, because the charges against them are lighter. However, they're obliged to come every day and sit in front of the box of the accused. The other eleven are accomplices in the attacks to varying degrees: while some are thought to be implicated up to their necks, for others things aren't so cut and dry. Here are some notes I've drawn up on each one:

The defendants

Salah Abdeslam, the star of the trial. Born and raised in Molenbeek, a district of Brussels reputed to be a haven for radicalised Muslims. The younger brother of Brahim Abdeslam, who blew himself up at the brasserie Le Comptoir Voltaire. Salah was supposed to blow himself up as well, and it's unclear whether his explosive belt didn't go off or if he thought better of it at the last minute. Only he can say. Will he?

Mohamed Abrini, a childhood friend of Salah Abdeslam's, also from Molenbeek. He seconded Abdeslam in the logistical preparations and was part of what he himself called 'the death convoy': the SEAT, VW Polo and Renault Clio in which the ten members of the commando travelled from Charleroi in Belgium to Paris on 12 November.

Osama Krayem, a Swedish national who came back from Syria in the late summer of 2015 to participate in attacks in Paris and Brussels. A seasoned fighter, he's thought to be the most senior Islamic State operative in the box.

Sofien Ayari, same profile as Osama Krayem. Returned with him from Syria, arrested with Salah Abdeslam on 18 March 2016. As they shot at their arresting officers, he's already been sentenced to 20 years in prison in Belgium and will be tried again at a later date for the attacks that left 32 dead and 340 injured in the Brussels metro and airport on 22 March 2016. In a general way, the trials of the attacks in Paris and Brussels – the latter being scheduled to take place in autumn 2022 – overlap.

Several of the Paris defendants also stand accused in Brussels, and they'll go from one trial to the next.

Mohamed Bakkali, logistics coordinator, in charge notably of renting hideouts in Brussels. In summer 2015 he took part in a foiled attack on a Thalys high-speed train for which he too has been given a heavy prison sentence – 25 years – in Belgium.

Adel Haddadi and **Muhammad Usman** left Syria in the summer of 2015 with the two Iraqis who blew themselves up at the Stade de France. Also Islamic State fighters, they should have taken part in the attacks but were arrested and imprisoned on their way, first on the Greek island of Kos, and then in Salzburg.

To varying degrees, the following people can be considered less directly involved. While the prosecution will try to establish that they knowingly assisted in the attacks, their lawyers will counter that they didn't know what they were doing and so deserve lighter sentences, or no sentence at all.

Yassine Atar's name appears in a series of messages found in a computer that contained details of the commando's plans. The brother of Osama Atar – who's presumed dead in Syria and is thought to be the brain behind the attacks – he never stops repeating that Osama is Osama and Yassine is Yassine, and that he, Yassine, has nothing to do with all of this.

Ali El Haddad Asufi is said to have helped procure the weapons. His participation remains unclear.

Farid Kharkhach provided the fake IDs. He admits to being a forger but not a terrorist, and swears he didn't know what he was getting himself into.

Mohammed Amri, Hamza Attou and **Ali Oulkadi** are the three friends from Molenbeek who helped exfiltrate Salah Abdeslam from Paris to Brussels on the morning of 14 November. Amri is also accused of renting cars with Abdeslam before the attacks: this explains why he is in the box while the other two appear as free individuals.

Abdellah Chouaa, finally, is accused of having had suspicious contacts with Mohamed Abrini during a trip the latter made to Syria in the summer of 2015. He also appears free.

A matter of names

One detail struck me in the biographies compiled in the OMA. Jihadi soldiers give themselves noms de guerre, or aliases, which are called *kunya*. They start with Abu, meaning father, and end with al-something, depending on the origin of the bearer. For example, Abu Bakr al-Baghdadi, the head of the Islamic State, chose the name because he was from Baghdad – and also because Abu Bakr was one of the Prophet's first companions. It was following this prestigious example that a young cyber-jihadist from Normandy whose first and last names were as French as can be gave himself the name Abu Ziyad al-Normandi. Four of the nine members of the commandos that carried out the attacks on 13 November were Belgian, so they called themselves al-Belgiki. Three were French: al-Faransi. Two were Iraqi: al-Iraqi. But if we consider the fourteen on trial here we no longer find any of these noms de guerre; they just go by their ho-hum everyday names. Some have nicknames, but it's not at all the same thing. Ahmed Dahmani – who's not on trial here because he's alreading doing time in Turkey – is also known as 'Gégé' or 'Prothèse', Mohamed Abrini also goes by 'Brink's' or 'Brioche'. At what point did the commandos receive or give themselves their jihadist handles, which they must have found highly gratifying? At what point did the others prudently decline to seek one? Did it go without saying that the right to bear one came at the cost of your life? And what about the defendant who remained irresolute, somewhere between the two groups? Unlike the others with him in the box, Salah Abdeslam had to kill and be killed. He did neither. And as if to underscore this unresolved status he too has an alias, but a truncated one: Abu Abderrahman. No particle, no title of murderous nobility, just that: Abu Abderrahman al-nothing at all.

Temporary worker

During the six years that the investigation has been under way he's refused to utter so much as a word, and the question on everyone's lips on this first day is: will he persist in his silence? If so, the trial will lose in interest. We lay odds; most of my colleagues are pessimistic. The roll call starts with him, again respecting alphabetical order. The presiding judge asks him to stand and state his civil status. Will he stand? Will he answer? He stands up. A youthful figure, his face is largely covered by his mask and the Salafist beard under it. Before any questions can be asked he recites in a loud voice the *shahada*, the grand, sober Islamic creed: 'There is no God but Allah, and Muhammad is his messenger.' A moment goes by. 'Well,' says the presiding judge, 'we'll see about that in due course. The names of your father and mother?' 'My father's and mother's names are no business of this court.' 'Profession?' 'Islamic State fighter.' The judge looks at his notes and says placidly: 'It says here: temporary worker.'

The plaintiffs

Victims by ricochet, unfortunate witnesses

'Wounded, bereaved, impacted': these are the plaintiffs, whose hearings will begin in late September. Several dozen are here already, on their benches which occupy more than half the room. Those with badges hanging from a red cord do not want to talk to the press, those with green cords indicate that they're not opposed to doing so. Some, undecided, wear both. For the moment it's mostly their lawyers we see. Bustling swarms of black robes. Here too the court calls the roll, and each lawyer comes forth in turn to declare for whom they are acting. For those already registered, this roll call is a mere formality. Nevertheless it lasts for two days, after which it's time for new plaintiffs to come forward, which they can do right up until the last minute. The court must then decide: which of these late candidates are admissible for victim status? which are not? In some cases there can be no doubt. The harm suffered by the bereaved and physically injured is clear. It's quantifiable, according to a scale that may seem monstrous but which exists and can be referred to for guidance: losing a sister pays more than losing a cousin, losing a leg more than losing a foot. In other cases it's debatable. To what extent, when you're neither injured nor bereaved, can you declare yourself 'impacted'? A well-dressed man approaches the stand. He claims to be a victim because he was at the Stade de France, where the attacks began. 'Inside or outside the stadium?' Judge Périès asks. 'Inside,' the man reluctantly admits. The problem, Périès says kindly, is that nothing happened inside the stadium. The terrorists *planned* to go in to blow themselves up, it's true. But as things turned out they didn't, and one cannot reasonably consider the 80,000 spectators of the friendly football match played that evening between France and Germany as victims of an assassination attempt. The same goes for those living near the Bataclan who saw dead or dying people on the pavement and still have nightmares about it today. It's not a matter of denying the reality of these nightmares, the sick leaves they've caused or the traumas they've induced, it's just that jurisprudence distinguishes between 'real' victims on the one hand, and 'victims by ricochet' and 'unfortunate witnesses' on the other, whose damages unfortunately cannot be compensated, otherwise there would be no end to the proceedings. One story circulating among the legal correspondents has to do with a woman who's demanding compensation because the attacks ruined her birthday party, which cost a fortune and was ages in the planning. It seems the story is true, but the woman didn't show up.

The Bataclan fabulist

Other stories deal with fake victims. Such people exist; in fact, there have been many. The journalist Alexandre Kauffmann wrote a book about one*, in which he vividly describes the community that grew up in the aftermath of the attacks. In the bars near the Place de la Bastille, people went over and over every detail of the night of hell. Where they were at the time of the attack, whom they were with. That woman beside me under the table at La Belle Équipe, is she alive or dead? Who was the guy who handed me a survival blanket when I made it to the far end of the Passage Amelot? Does anyone know? Does anyone know anyone who knows? Legends took shape. There'd been stabbings at the Bataclan, people said, bodies had been mutilated, a pregnant woman had had her guts ripped open, a man's penis had been hacked off, there'd been a fourth attacker – only it was decided on high that no one should know about him. These Arabian nights of horror were recounted again and again in real time, in the streets and cafés, but also and above all online. In December 2015, a childminder who was at the Bataclan with her husband launched what would become the association Life for Paris on her Facebook page. Very quickly it attracted hundreds of survivors and bereaved. One of the many

* *La Mythomane du Bataclan*, Éditions Goutte d'Or, 2021.

followers is a certain Flo. She's not a direct victim, but she's dedicated heart and soul to helping Greg, her best friend, who was gravely wounded and is now laid up at Georges Pompidou Hospital . . . The craziest thing, she repeats, is that whereas Greg never went to the Bataclan, she went there all the time: she was supposed to go that evening and then she didn't feel up to it, she changed her mind at the last minute, she'd been that close to going. There are people like that, who brag their whole lives about how they came two minutes late for a plane that crashed. Hard-working and with time on her hands, Flo becomes the forum's webmaster. She welcomes, guides, assists and comforts visitors, and posts initiatives and events organised by the community – outings, birthdays, commemorations on the Boulevard Voltaire where crowds gather in front of candles, flowers, photos and drawings. When people marvel at her empathy, she says the ordeal has allowed her to mature and become more open to others. It even lets her forget the cruel disease she suffers from: Cushing's syndrome, which has made her obese and hairy. Flo is so efficient at Life for Paris that she's asked to join the managing board. In this capacity she addresses the French National Assembly regarding a bill on aid to the victims, then poses together with the association's most high-profile figures for *Paris Match* magazine. Under the heading 'Lasting trauma', the lead paragraph reads: 'They manage to smile – and even go back to the bar where it happened.' Another photo shows her in a leather jacket, clearly in more rock'n'roll

mode, in the arms of Jesse Hughes, the lead singer of
the Eagles of Death Metal – the band that played at the
Bataclan on 13 November 2015, and which returned for
a memorial concert at the Olympia the following February. Along with representing the victims and offering
psychological support, her new gig, as she puts it, also
involves distinguishing between real survivors and the
many dodgy characters who gravitate towards other
people's misfortune. In this respect her radar is infal-
lible. On the French version of the *Got Talent* series, a
secondary school student dedicated his song to Alexandre, his best friend who died at the Bataclan. As it turns
out no one called Alexandre died at the Bataclan. The
student got caught in a web of lies, amid the growing
condemnation of the social networks and of Flo, who
says she was the first to see through the scam and writes
on the forum: 'Bull-shit. The only reason he did this was
to up his audience ratings, it's disgusting to use tragic
events like that . . .' Not long afterwards she'll be
unmasked in her turn, because while continuing to speak
in Greg's name, she proceeds to declare herself a victim
as well. Her statement is one of the most complete, precise and convincing accounts of the night of horror at
the Bataclan. Nevertheless suspicions are aroused, and
these become more tangible when a member of the
association bumps into her in the waiting room of a
therapist specialised in survivors' disorders. Checks, cross-
checks. Finally it comes out that there is no one called
Greg among the patients at Georges Pompidou Hospital,

or on the list of victims, but that Flo, for her part, has received 25,000 euros in compensation – and that's just an advance. Arthur Dénouveaux, the president of Life for Paris, presses charges, but he does so with some reluctance because he likes her and, he says, because from the depths of her loneliness Flo found in their group of survivors the first real friends she's ever had. Tried for fraud and breach of trust, Flo is sentenced to four years in prison. The epigraph to Alexandre Kauffmann's book is a sentence by Christine Villemin, the mother of little Grégory and heroine of the Grégory Affair – another crime story that captivated French public attention in the 1980s: 'It seems people are envious of our misfortune.'

The jackal

Defence of rupture?

On the second day, while the plaintiffs were still coming forward, it was announced that the victims' testimonies would soon be heard. Suddenly Salah Abdeslam stood up in the box, made signs until his microphone was turned on, and asked if we'd also be hearing from those who'd been bombed in Syria and Iraq. That would be discussed in due course, the presiding judge responded, and switched off his microphone. In general the comment was seen as a provocation. Still, it left me thinking. It invokes the so-called 'defence of rupture', introduced in 1987 by the famous and hugely provocative lawyer Jacques Vergès during the trial of the Nazi officer Klaus Barbie. Granted, said Vergès, Barbie tortured prisoners in Lyon during the German occupation of France, but the French Army did the same in Algeria in the sixties. So every time the topic of torture in Lyon was brought up, Vergès's defence focused on the torture in Algeria. While I would be surprised if Olivia Ronen, Abdeslam's very young lawyer, went as far as emulating Jacques Vergès, it is true that the French Army tortured in Algeria, even if that doesn't put it on a par with the SS. And it's true that the international coalition to which France belonged dropped bombs on Iraq – and on Syria starting in 2014 – causing dozens, perhaps hundreds, of civilian casualties – because 'surgical strikes' are a myth. I was all the more surprised while going over the order of indictment – which everyone agrees is rigorous and extremely well put together – to find a reference to '*alleged* civilian massacres *said to be committed* by the West in the course of the bombings'. I'm no expert, and I won't deal here with the subject of whether the death of half a million Iraqi children directly caused by US sanctions was 'worth it', as former US Secretary of State Madeleine Albright said in a memorable interview; however, it serves neither the truth nor justice to call indisputable civilian massacres '*alleged* civilian massacres'. Nor does it serve the interests of justice and truth to deny that Salah Abdeslam's conditions of detention are extremely harsh. Six years in solitary confinement is harsh indeed, as Olivia Ronen underscored at the first hearing. The young man who had just entered the box like a bull in the arena had hardly spoken to anyone for six years, she said, and it was her duty to say so. I listened to her, I agreed with her, at the same time I thought about the email that Frank Berton, Abdeslam's previous lawyer, received after complaining that his client was under video surveillance 24/7:

Dear sir,

Ever since her evening at the Bataclan, my daughter-in-law has also been under video surveillance 24 hours a day, in the hospital.

This situation doesn't trouble her, because she's in a deep coma.

Nor does it trouble my son, who lies in the cemetery.

I respect your work and your convictions, but there are limits when faced with people's suffering.

A ghost from the past

As the 'V13 liner' – as we all, magistrates, lawyers and journalists, have come to call this mega trial of Friday 13 November – slowly cruises along, it's business as usual at the courthouse. In a small courtroom in the basement, another special criminal court is trying another terrorist. This trial attracts little attention. A lawyer friend drew my attention to it, and we went down to take a break from the parade of plaintiffs. The defendant is an old man in a sky-blue suit with a matching scarf and handkerchief, slicked-back white hair, a thin moustache and a strong Spanish accent. From his glass box he warmly welcomes what seems to be a faithful audience comprising, in order of appearance: an old fan for whom he signs an autograph: 'Revolutionary greetings'; two guys in elegant suits who look like bankers and who, despite their appearance, identify themselves as members of the yellow vests protest movement; two nice old ladies, militant supporters of the Palestinian cause since way back when, one of whom takes a manifestly antisemitic pamphlet from her handbag and gives it to the other; a young man in a tracksuit clutching far-right politician Éric Zemmour's latest book tightly to his chest; and, to round things off, the Right Reverend Jacques Gaillot – the leftist former bishop who was often in the news, as some may recall, towards the end of the nineties. They all know each other, the defendant has a kind word for each one. Seeing one of the nice old antisemites kissing the old fan on the cheek, he jokes: 'Fooling around behind my back, are you?' His lawyer Isabelle Coutant-Peyre, a tall, skinny woman with charcoal-coloured hair and eyes who also happens to be his wife, arrives balancing three cups of coffee: one for her husband, one for her, and one for the public prosecutor. She gives it to him, also joking: 'Bribe, anyone?' The prosecutor smiles, clearly the two go way back. This is the third time he's acted against the defendant, she's defended him seven times. The issue at stake in the trial is the length of the sentence he faces for the grenade attack on Publicis Drugstore in Paris (1974, two dead, thirty-four wounded), although the proceedings are purely procedural because he's long since been sentenced to life several times over for his many other crimes. He's been in prison for twenty-seven years, he'll end his days there, it's just that this trial will be his last, no more appeals are possible, meaning that this is the final bow of Ilich Ramírez Sánchez, aka Carlos the Jackal. It's not a joke: a few flights down from V13, and without arousing any more interest than that of his fan club, *Carlos* is on trial. Carlos, the legendary terrorist of the 1970s. Carlos, the most famous client of defence lawyer Jacques Vergès. In his opening words the prosecutor could not resist making a connection with what was going on upstairs, recalling that it was Carlos who committed the first indiscriminate murders on French soil, also bloody attacks. When Coutant-Peyre pleaded it was unconstrained, freewheeling. She told anecdotes, recalled memories, he interrupted her, she said, 'If you know better than I do, you go ahead and plead,' whereupon he grumbled and sat back down. This incredibly strange scene was pure comedy, and my lawyer friend and I couldn't help laughing up our sleeves. But we would have laughed less if, there in the courtroom facing this ghost of vintage terrorism in bell-bottoms and these picturesque clowns, there had been a woman in a wheelchair who'd been a little girl in 1974, who'd gone with her parents for an ice-cream cone at Publicis Drugstore and whose life was devastated that day.

Major facial trauma

Two hours, thirty-eight minutes and forty-seven seconds

Those who attended the *Charlie Hebdo* trial eight months ago will not forget the trauma of the photos taken at the crime scene. The newsroom, the bodies. And then by the surveillance video. The entrance hall, the assassins entering, one of the two Kouachi brothers standing guard while the other kills: one minute and forty-nine seconds that many would rather not have seen. In agreement with the presiding judge, the police officers who sketched a sort of inventory of the crime scenes throughout the second week of V13 made the opposite choice: to spare the plaintiffs and keep what they showed to a minimum. Photos, but taken from a distance. Charts and diagrams. The devastated but empty terrace of the café Le Carillon. A litany of names, chalk outlines on the pavements, numbered yellow or blue markers called ID tents, but no bloody bodies. Relatively few images, hardly any sound. And yet there are audio files. A spectator at the Bataclan was recording the concert on a Dictaphone which was later found. It kept recording all during the massacre, resulting in an audio tape which, from the arrival of the terrorist commando to the final police assault, lasts two

hours, thirty-eight minutes and forty-seven seconds.
The question naturally arose as to whether it should be
played to those present. Here, too, the court decided in
favour of discretion, playing only the first twenty-two
seconds. The band Eagles of Death Metal plays. The first
gunshots blend in with the drums. Feedback screeches,
the sound is immediately cut. During the break, a young
woman who was at the Bataclan that night told me what
she had a right to say and I did not: 'That wasn't enough.
If it was supposed to give any idea of what it was like in
there, it's not enough. It's as good as nothing.' I don't
know. In a week's time, others who were there will begin
to put words to what it was like. In the meantime, the
investigator who made the initial findings testifies. He's
a police officer who must have seen a lot in his twenty
years on the crime brigade, but he trembled as he spoke.
'What you didn't hear,' he said, 'the remaining two hours,
thirty-eight minutes and twenty-five seconds, was tran-
scribed by an officer, word for word, sound for sound,
shot for shot – 258 shots in burst fire and then shot by
shot for the first thirty-two minutes.' How long it took
the officer to do this is unclear. One would rather not
imagine what his nights were like. And since the killers
spoke at the beginning, and since the court had to hear
their words without listening to the tape, it was the police
officer himself, Patrick Bourbotte, who read them out.
He said: 'I'll have to speak the terrorists' words. It's not
the easiest thing I've had to do in my career as a judicial
police officer.' His voice shook, then he took a gulp of

air and began to read, bravely, changing his voice like an apprentice actor as he read the parts of 'assailant number one' Fouad Mohamed Aggad, 'assailant number two' Omar Ismael Mostefai and 'assailant number three' Samy Amimour:

'. . . *You can blame your president François Hollande . . . He's playing the cowboy, like in a western, bombing our brothers in Syria and Iraq, we're here to pay you back . . .'*

'We soldiers of the caliphate are everywhere in the world. We'll strike everywhere . . .'

'Hey, you, don't move.'

A shot.

'I said, don't move.'

Seventeen body parts

On the morning of 14 November 2015, two victims were mixed up in the morgue. The parents of one believed their daughter was dead although she was alive, those of the other hoped like mad that she was alive although she was dead. Called to testify, the head of the morgue explained: the situation was unprecedented – the arrival in just a few hours of '123 whole bodies and seventeen body parts'. 'Seventeen body parts': this is the kind of thing heard day after day by the people of all ages sitting on the benches reserved for them. Some of them already know each other, others are alone: the plaintiffs of V13. For some these body parts belonged to the children, the men or the women they loved. Other terms they'll get to know by heart: laceration, dismemberment, poly-perforation caused by the nuts, bolts and screws packed into the suicide vests. Scatter zone: this being the fifty-metre radius out from the centre of an explosion in which human remains are found. The words of the Research and Intervention Brigade investigator who was among the first to enter the Bataclan: 'We walked among the tangled, twisted, overlapping bodies, I don't know what the correct term is. We slipped in pools of blood, crushed teeth and bones beneath our feet, phones were vibrating, families were calling. When we started to evacuate the bodies they were so soaked in blood, so heavy, that it took four of us to lift just one. I was ter-rified that we could pass a victim hidden away in some mouse hole who'd die without being seen. A good two weeks later we found another one of the terrorists' legs.' When a lawyer acting on behalf of the plaintiffs asked the investigator who did the same job at the café La Belle Équipe the odd question of how he 'felt' about the kill-ings, he answered: 'How I felt? I don't know. I can only tell you that there were thirty holes in one victim, twenty-two in another, fourteen in a third.' And: 'You have to understand that the damage done with a 7.62 mm calibre projectile isn't the same as with 9 mm. 9 mm calibre bullets leave holes with an entrance and an exit wound. 7.62 mm calibre bullets leave gaping flesh wounds, exploded skulls, major facial traumas.'

Another thing the victims' friends and relatives will have learned: in forensic language a face that's severely mangled, sometimes to the point of being unrecognisable, is called 'a major facial trauma'.

Propaganda

The video put out by the Islamic State claiming responsibility for the attacks would be shown, however. In an expurgated version. But expurgated or not, its sheer atrocity leaves one speechless. Filmed, edited and set to music like a Hollywood blockbuster or a video game, it shows the 'nine lions of the caliphate' – the future Paris suicide bombers – training on a rocky landscape, probably somewhere in Syria, in the summer of 2015. They know that in a few months' time they will kill and die. For now they're beheading prisoners, one each. And not only are they beheading them, some laugh as they do it. The film lasts seventeen minutes, and it's pure propaganda. I may be wrong, but it strikes me that such propaganda is completely unprecedented. However awful its message may be, propaganda generally presents a virtuous face. Processions, young people gazing stalwartly towards a radiant future. Nazi propaganda didn't show Auschwitz, Stalinist propaganda didn't show the gulag, Khmer Rouge propaganda didn't show the S-21 torture centre. Normally propaganda hides horror. Here it puts it on show. The Islamic State doesn't say: this is war, sadly for good to triumph we must commit terrible acts. No, it lauds itself for its sadism. It uses sadism, displays of sadism, and the permission to be sadistic to recruit.

'It's not a joke'

Before emerging from Rue Bichat, the SEAT carrying the trio that would spray the terraces of Le Carillon and Le Petit Cambodge with bullets stopped at a red light across from two passers-by, who describe the scene. One of the terrorists lowered his window and said: 'The Islamic State has come to slit your throats.' Then as he drove off he added: 'It's not a joke.'

Maia, Le Carillon

'I met Amine while we were studying architecture,' Maia says. 'He became my friend, then my lover, then my husband, then my business partner. We created our office together. He was my first love, he was my love. We had projects. We talked about our lives, the kids we'd have. We got married twice. The first time in Paris in 2014, the second in 2015 in Morocco, in Rabat, where he grew up and where his family lives. We met Émilie, who became a very good friend of ours, and then her twin sister Charlotte. They were beautiful, very close, we laughed a lot. There was also Mehdi, Amine's childhood friend. All five of us were architects. We met every Friday evening at Le Carillon, not far from the office. We didn't need to make a date, it went without saying. That evening the weather was so mild that we sat outside, on the terrace. It felt like spring had come early, people seemed happy just to be walking in the streets. I remember thinking that life was good and that we were lucky. When it started we were talking about our birthdays. I was twenty-seven, the others were twenty-nine, we were wondering what we'd do to celebrate the four of them turning thirty. And then it happened.'

(A very long pause.)

'So, what did happen . . . It's all a jumble. The noises, the bangs we thought were firecrackers at first, the smell of gunpowder. I had no idea, but the smell of gunpowder is horrible. I thought Amine, Émilie and Charlotte were hiding under the table – in fact they'd been gunned down. I dived onto the street, between the pavement and the wheels of a car. I curled up to avoid the bullets but they hit me anyway, in the legs. I felt the shocks in my body. Terrible, wrenching shocks, I didn't know then that it was the expanding bullets lacerating my legs. I hadn't yet learned the term 'gunshot laceration'. I didn't feel the pain, not yet. At one point I feel death behind me. There's a guy right up close, pressed against my back. I hear him gasp and wheeze, I know these are his last moments. I know that I'm experiencing the last moments of his life. It's something very intimate, perhaps the most intimate thing you can share with someone. I can't see him, he's behind me, but I feel his breath, I hear him. I'm the only witness to his death. I will never know his name.

'Death comes, and with it silence. And then I hear the groaning, the moaning, the first words of the rescue workers: "Conscious people first, take care of the conscious people first." I manage to sit up, I don't know how. I look around for Amine. He's lying on the ground among the other bodies. He fell on his back. I can see his face, I see that his eyes are open, and I know he's gone. It's not the blood, it's not the twenty-two bullets that I don't yet know hit his lungs, his liver and his heart, all I can see are his eyes and they're empty. Vacuous. He's dead. I can also see Émilie and Charlotte but I can't get any closer for now because Amine's body is in the way. Mehdi hasn't moved. He's still at the table where the five of us had been sitting. He's alive, he's wounded, there's a lot of blood on his T-shirt. I ask if he's okay. He says yes, I'm okay, in a weirdly normal voice, adding, you need help. I see blood running down my legs, and then I see that parts of my legs are missing. I reach down and try to stick my left calf back where it belongs. Someone hands me a cloth, I try to make tourniquets, above my left knee, around my right shin. I was taken to Bichat Hospital, and from there I called my mother. I told her I was alive, adding: "I think Amine's dead." That's a lie, I don't *think* Amine's dead, I *know* he's dead. This lie will give Amine's mother hope that will last until the next afternoon. I'm sorry for that, even today. Then I was transferred to Ambroise Paré Hospital, where the first operations took place in the emergency department so that I wouldn't lose my leg. The hours that followed, the first nights in the hospital, are impossible to describe. There was the fear. The first fits of tears. I've always thought of myself as quite a strong person, not a victim at all. But there I didn't think it was humanly possible to feel such distress and loneliness. There would be four operations in all. What kept me going were my legs. I was twenty-seven, I had my whole life to live, I needed my legs. I had to be able to get up and stand. Today, as you see, I am standing, happy to be standing, happy to walk without crutches or knee braces.

'Amine was buried in Morocco while I was still in hospital. I wasn't able to go to his funeral. I did even less for Charlotte and Émilie. I've never visited their graves. They were my dearest friends and since they died I've neglected them. Amine took up too much room in my heart, there was none left for them. There were five of us, now only two are left. At first I thought Mehdi and I would help each other out, but that's not what happened. He disappeared from my life, we went our separate ways, I think it was too much for him. I didn't hear from him after that. There were five of us, now I'm alone.

'I work. I've had to rethink my career. Recently I won a contract in a fairly large town, it's a big job. I left Paris and found a lover who can put up with the person I've become. There, that's been my struggle, tending to my wounds one by one. It's been six years now. It's exhausting. I hold my head high but I'm exhausted. I know there are things that won't come back. I won't run any more. I no longer dream. My nights have become barren. I have doubts about my work. I'm not as reliable as I once was. My friends are gone forever. What I'd like now is to live, just to live. To love without feeling guilty. To enjoy a carefree evening with friends. To accept new hardships, like my father's illness. To stop being afraid of losing everything.

'The trial has put me on hold. I've been waiting for a year. I wish I didn't need to be here but I do. I'd have liked to get my life in order and not think about all this, but that wouldn't be possible. What do I expect? Punishment that fits the crime. Justice. It won't change anything for me, but it's good that this trial is taking place. That's all. Thank you for listening.'

'First see to the living'

The acrobat and the rugby player

Alice and Aristide are brother and sister. They look alike: black hair, sculpted faces, slender bodies, both very attractive. She was twenty-three, he was twenty-six. She's a professional circus artist: an acrobat. Her work consists of leaping backwards in the air, her hands clasped in those of a lifter, but she puts it differently: 'My job is to make people dream with my arms.' Aristide is a rugby player, also professional. He plays and lives in Italy. Both are top athletes. Their rigorous training schedules leave them little time to see each other, so this meet-up for dinner in Paris is a celebration. They go to Le Petit Cambodge, opposite Le Carillon, because the bobuns are so good there, but that evening the terrace is packed and so is the restaurant, so they mill around for a bit while coming up with a plan B. Then the car with tinted windows pulls up and a guy who looks a lot like one of Aristide's best friends gets out, except that he's got a Kalashnikov which he raises and starts shooting. Alice didn't see any of this, she just heard the first shots, already she's on the ground. With his rugby reflexes Aristide throws himself on top of her and protects her with his whole body. It's chaos, it's deafening, there's no telling whether it's seconds or minutes that go by. At one point she feels a pain she could never have imagined existed, her arm must have jutted out from under Aristide, who takes three of these monstrous bullets. Alice will say that Aristide saved her life by throwing himself on her. Aristide will say that Alice saved his life by managing, in the chaos of moaning, dying and attempts at first aid, to get him taken to the hospital where he's diagnosed as being 'on the verge of death'. She was operated on twice in the same night, in two different hospitals, and then five more times, which saved her arm without letting her use it again. Aristide had lung injuries and extensive brain damage and was told that although his right leg was saved – that is, it would not be amputated – he would not walk again. A few months later he was walking, he even tried to run, but the pain and distress were so great that he spent months in a psychiatric hospital. Coming to terms with no longer playing rugby was a long and painful process. Even today he can't go near a TV showing a match: the sadness overwhelms him. Alice is also disabled, she can no longer support herself with her arms. 'But I keep working as an acrobat,' she says. 'I invent new moves with my lifters by balancing on my feet. I want to go on making people dream. It's difficult. It's difficult,' she repeats. There's a silence, her chin trembles, her mouth twitches, and out of this twitch comes a miraculous smile. The two of them also say what everyone else says: they suffer from hypervigilance, nightmares, the irrevocable loss of innocence. But they also say they're thankful: in a way luck was on their side, they're alive. They struggle, but against no one. For themselves, with themselves, with others. This isn't positive-thinking doublespeak, it's a truth they've paid dearly for the right to say. Aristide: 'I tried to understand how young people could get it into their heads to shoot other young people like that. I don't understand, maybe there's nothing to understand. But I'm happy that they can be questioned. I'm happy this trial is taking place. I think that my generation and the one after us have a tre- mendous need to believe in justice.' He glances over to his left at the box holding the accused, then turns away. He faces the court in front of him, standing very straight on his two legs. We look at the two of them, Alice and him. The fact that they're here, talking to us, is already justice.

The accent of truth

This trial has the colossal ambition of seeking to unfold, over a period of nine months, from every angle, from the point of view of everyone involved, what happened that night. The first two weeks were spent inventorying the situation. Police officers, gendarmes, doctors came and described what they'd seen. These hardened men wept as they spoke. Now we're entering a new phase. For the next five weeks we'll hear the testimonies of the plaintiffs, that is of the survivors and the relatives of the dead. Those to whom this thing *happened*. The testimonies are frighteningly intense, and there are around fifteen of them per day. They started four days ago – it feels like it's been a month already. The hearings start at half past noon and are supposed to end at 7.30 p.m., though they often last longer. And since it's complicated to leave the building because you have to go through the security check all over again when you come back in, we hardly see the light of day: at 6 p.m. it could just as well be 3 a.m. Other things fade away. Having dinner with friends would be a non-starter. The presiding judge, whose affable firmness we've come to appreciate, made a slip of the tongue for which he immediately apologised: so as not to burden the court and to 'avoid repetition', he said, the plaintiffs' lawyers should confer with each other and their clients. Just what would that mean, to 'avoid repetition'? Of course there are things that all those who were on the terraces – since we're dealing with the terraces this week – say. That they first thought it was firecrackers, then that they were caught in a settling of scores, before grasping the crazy fact: men with war weapons had got out of a car *to kill them*. That when it stopped, when the car had left, there was what we sometimes unthinkingly call *a deathly silence*, only it *really was* a deathly silence: only after some time did the screaming start. That it was sheer carnage, a butchery, a tangle of bodies with huge holes out of which blood, flesh and organs oozed, and that when the first-aid workers arrived they repeated: 'First see to the living.' But there is no repetition and there cannot be any either, because every-one experienced these same moments with their own history, their own complications, their own deaths, and they're now describing them in their own words. They're not facts that can be reeled off, but voices that unfold, and all of them – well, almost all of them – ring true. Almost all of them have the accent of truth. That is what makes this long string of testimonies not only terrible but also magnificent, and it is not out of morbid curiosity that we who follow the trial would not trade places for anything in the world, or even think of missing a day. I've read, heard and sometimes thought that we live in a victim society, one which is happy to confuse the status of victim and hero. That may be; nevertheless a large number of the victims we hear from day after day do strike me as heroes. Because of the courage it took them to rebuild their lives, their way of living this experience, and the strength of the ties that bind them to the dead and to the living. On rereading these lines I realise that they sound overblown, but I don't know how to say it otherwise: as these young people – because yes, almost all of them are young – take the stand one after the next, we see their souls. And we come out grateful, shocked and feeling as though we have matured with them.

Nadia

Twenty-four hours passed between the last time Nadia Mondeguer saw her daughter, at 2 p.m. on Friday, and the moment she learned of her death, at 2 p.m. on Saturday, and it was these twenty-four hours that she came to describe to the court, minute by minute. Nadia has dishevelled grey hair, a lined face, the voice of a heavy smoker and a very slight accent that's hard to pin down. When she talks, we listen. She'll talk for a long time, we'll listen for a long time. For lunch on the 13th she'd prepared a cauliflower gratin she was not at all displeased with, she says, and she'll never make a cauliflower gratin again. Lamia only showed up at the last minute, as she often did. For the past four years she'd been living with her friend Louise on Rue Bréguet, but she'd kept the keys to her parents' flat on Boulevard Voltaire, and as it was just a stone's throw away she sometimes dropped by unannounced. Her brother Yohann was there and the three of them had lunch. They joked around at first, then as it was Friday the 13th they wondered if they should be worried. No need, they decided; still Lamia said: 'I don't know, this Friday the 13th kind of gives me the creeps. As if it really was unlucky.' She had a sore back. In her last post she asked if anyone could recommend a good and cheap osteopath. 'My back thanks you,' she wrote. Nadia adds: She was shot in the back.

Lamia's in a hurry, she runs off saying to Nadia: Let's have lunch together next week. It's a ritual they have, ever since she left home and has been earning a living, Lamia has made a point of treating her mother and father to lunch in turns. She goes home to change before meeting one of her actresses at 4 p.m. – she's a talent agent. At 6.30 p.m. she attends her friend Francis's thesis defence at the Conservatoire des Arts et Métiers. It's there, at 7.21 p.m., that the last photo of her is taken. It's projected onto the same screen where the crime scenes were shown the day before. Leaning against a yellow wall, she's talking to two people with their backs to the camera and has just noticed a third, the one taking the picture. She's turned towards the camera and is smiling. She has brown, shoulder-length hair parted in the middle and a large mouth. She's thirty but there's something childlike about her. She radiates beauty, joy and kindness. She makes me think of my daughter, and of how she might be in fifteen years. Drinks are served after the thesis defence, some of those present will go on to celebrate a friend's birthday near the Gare de Lyon, but Lamia can't go along because she's arranged to see Romain. She met Romain a few months earlier. On 21 October she brought him for dinner on Boulevard Voltaire. Nadia immediately felt at ease with this tall, blond, blue-eyed man from the Sancerre region, who played rugby and had opened a café across from the Musée de

Cluny, where, he suggested in passing, Nadia could come and have breakfast with him later that week if she liked. Deal? – Deal. Charmed, Nadia thought: he's the one. The last text message in Lamia's mobile is from Romain. He has no preference about where they should meet up and writes: *You decide.* Lamia chooses La Belle Équipe, a café they both like. Romain has settled into the neighbourhood and lives just ten minutes away. At 8.30 p.m. Lamia says goodbye to her friends, takes the metro to Arts et Métiers station and arrives at La Belle Équipe at 8.50 p.m. The customers are young, they drink beer and mojitos and nibble on platters of cheese or charcuterie. It's mild, there's a lively atmosphere and quite a crowd – it came out later that two birthdays were being celebrated that evening. Lamia still manages to find a table on the terrace – near the window separating La Belle Équipe from a Japanese restaurant. Romain joins her ten minutes later. They have thirty-five minutes left to live, and Nadia likes to think that they lived these thirty-five minutes under the spell of the first moments of love. Another photo, showing them together a few weeks earlier, suggests they did.

Nadia, meanwhile, spends the afternoon on WhatsApp, following a family reunion in honour of her niece who lives in Turkey. She should have gone to the theatre in the northern suburb of Gennevilliers with the four students she teaches Arabic to, but her husband Jean-François has just come back from the Hôpital Saint-Louis where he's had a urinary catheter inserted.

The intervention was painful; he's tough but exhausted. Nadia decides to stay home with him and calls her students to say she can't make it. After dinner Jean-François lies down on their bed. Yohann goes to his room to watch the France–Germany football match that's being played at the Stade de France. Nadia stays in the living room and clicks her way around the website of the Arab World Institute, which she knows almost inside out. She looks over the music programme and listens to some nasheeds.

At the word nasheed a rustle goes through the crowd. It comes up regularly in the investigators' statements; the lawyers repeat it as if they'd known it forever. Nasheeds are chants referencing Islamic beliefs, and also hold a firm place in jihadist culture. Musically they're more or less like rap, the lyrics are often belligerent, bloodthirsty even, but it must not be forgotten, Nadia stresses, that the songs stem from the Sufi tradition and are an expression of the loftiest Muslim spirituality: the Gregorian chants of Islam. She's interested in them for a reason. Her family on her father's side are Christian Palestinians, and have lived in Egypt for two generations. She was born in Cairo, and it was there that she met Jean-François. A native of Brittany, he chose to teach French abroad rather than do military service at home, and from 1973 until his death in 2020 he was the great love of her life. When they moved to Paris in 1974, Jean-François got a job teaching migrant workers and she provided administrative assistance to the same migrant workers under the new integration policy put in place by then president Giscard d'Estaing. For fourteen years she worked with the social services in the suburb of Nanterre, helping immigrants with their official correspondence. There she experienced the last migrant slums before they were torn down to make room for council estates. Then when she was pregnant with Lamia she went back to school and studied history and Arabic, before teaching Arabic first at an institute of Egyptology and later at the Arab World Institute. Her master's thesis dealt with the Salafist journal founded in Cairo at the beginning of the twentieth century by the Syrian scholar Muhammad Rashid Rida, who inspired the Muslim Brotherhood. It's not getting off track to say that this association, born in the 1920s on the banks of the Suez Canal, invented what is known as Islamism – that is the idea that the rigorous application of Quranic law, the sharia, is the solution to all political and social problems and the remedy for the decline of the Arab countries – or that this is the origin of jihadism.

The three of them spend a quiet evening in the flat. The nasheeds answer the muffled clamour of the match Yohann is watching on the other side of the wall. At 9.30 p.m., their neighbour on the fifth floor calls to ask after Jean-François. 'He's very tired,' says Nadia, 'but he'll be okay.' In the meantime, she'll learn later, the SEAT which has already sprayed three terraces with bullets has turned onto the Avenue Parmentier and then the Boulevard Voltaire. It passed under their windows, perhaps even stopping at the light at the foot of their building, then continued three hundred metres to the Rue de Charonne, on the corner of which are two large and busy cafés. Nadia wondered a lot afterwards why they didn't commit their massacre right there, it would have been so much simpler than turning onto the Rue de Charonne and heading down to La Belle Équipe, which was smaller and couldn't even be seen from Boulevard Voltaire. One has to think that they'd scouted around and had a reason to choose La Belle Équipe – but what? At 9.35 p.m. Nadia hears a series of bangs from the streets behind the building. She leans out of the window to see if there's anything happening on the boulevard down below. She can still remember how police vans raced back and forth with their sirens blaring back in January, when *Charlie Hebdo* and the Hypercacher supermarket were attacked. But now there's nothing. Things stay calm for another half an hour. It's only at 10.16 p.m. that she receives an alarming message on WhatsApp. It's from her niece in Cairo, who tells them that there have been attacks in Paris. From that moment on the three of them follow events on the news. Mostly the reports concern the Bataclan, but also the terraces in the 11th arrondissement where they've been living for forty years – except for their elder son Gwendal, who's lived in Cairo for the past seven. Nadia calls Lamia again and again. She doesn't pick up, but she herself said that her phone had been on the blink since the day before: it's normal not to be able to reach her. The same goes for Romain. They're together: everything's fine.

Yohann nevertheless suggests calling the toll-free number that's been set up for families. Nadia hesitates. Calling would mean acknowledging that they're worried, whereas there's nothing to worry about. There's nothing to worry about, she repeats, and tells her husband and son a story they already know. It took place on 6 October 1981. Celebrations were under way in Cairo to mark the victory of the Egyptian Army over Israel which started the 1973 Yom Kippur War. Nadia's mother had just had an operation. Her father, who was a journalist at the French radio station in Cairo, drove Nadia to the hospital to visit her. On the way they passed the parade. Nadia's mother was recovering well, and the two spent the day chatting quietly at her bedside. Outside the window was a garden, they could hear birds. At one point they were surprised to hear a helicopter flying noisily overhead. It was only at nine in the evening that Nadia's sister arrived and told them that Egypt was in an uproar because President Anwar Sadat had been assassinated by members of the Egyptian Islamic Jihad. Nadia and her mother spent that peaceful day unaware of the great misfortune that had occurred, ruining all efforts for peace in the Middle East. Nadia clings to this memory, telling herself that if Lamia and Romain are unreachable, it's because they want to be and have turned off their phones. Paris may be all fire and blood, but they know nothing about it and wouldn't want to if they did. They're alone in the world, and happy.

Nadia finally did call the toll-free number, at around 2 a.m. The reassuring answer: there was no trace of Lamia among the victims. Of course they'll be called if there's any news. She dozes off in an armchair. By morning the crisis cell hasn't called, so it's with a certain degree of confidence that she posts a message of support for the victims' families on Facebook. At ten o'clock the four students in her Arabic class arrive. Aged between forty-five and seventy-eight, they come rain or shine. As soon as they understand the situation they want to leave again so as not to burden her with their presence, but Nadia asks them to stay and they sit there feeling increasingly ill at ease. Meanwhile Lamia's friends do the rounds of the hospitals. At 1 p.m. Romain's mother calls and tells Jean-François that Romain is dead: they've just received word. And it's at 2 p.m. that Romain's brother's fiancée calls and tells Jean-François: 'Monsieur Mondeguer, forgive me for being blunt: Lamia is on the lists.'

They're in the living room. Jean-François turns to Nadia. She remembers that he did not say: 'Lamia is dead,' but: 'Lamia is on the lists.'

'At that point,' Nadia tells the court, 'a trapdoor opens. We're sucked down into a dark hold. Above, on deck, things still move. We're no longer part of the world we were still in touch with just a few moments earlier. I didn't shout. I became unhitched. It was real and unreal. Jean-François said, "I'm sad." Just that: "I'm sad." And from his voice I understood that he was destroyed to the depths of his soul.'

At 3 p.m., after informing Gwendal, Jean-François went to the Paris Forensic Institute with Ylias, one of Lamia's oldest friends. They went by Uber, which wasn't yet common in those days, Jean-François had never heard of it. There they were told that she'd been shot at La Belle Équipe, 150 metres from their home. They were also told that both she and Romain had been killed instantly, they hadn't suffered. That's a consolation.

In the late afternoon, Ylias asked them if some of Lamia's friends could come and share their loss. They needed it. 'I put myself in their shoes,' says Nadia, 'I understood what they were going through.' She had no idea that so many would come: around thirty of them climbed the four flights of stairs and sat together in silence in the living room. On the sofa, on the chairs, on the floor. Jean-François and Nadia stayed in the bedroom. They couldn't hear a thing. There were thirty young people in the next room but they didn't hear a peep. At least on the first night. After that their visitors started talking. For almost two months they came back every day. They brought things to eat and drink, you could hear them coming up the stairs, the door was always open, the flat always full. They talked about Lamia, about their lives, about life. Most of them Nadia and Jean-François didn't know. They just knew her friends from primary school, which was two blocks away, and from her lycée. Lamia had been loyal, she'd even stayed friends with a girl from kindergarten. Now they met her more recent acquaintances, people from very different walks of life in which their daughter had moved with ease, cherished by all. It was a consolation to know how much she had been loved.

Late at night, once everyone had left, Jean-François and Nadia walked over to La Belle Équipe. Before the attack Nadia used to grumble about all the tables on the pavement when she walked by the café on her way to the post office. Now there were candles, drawings, messages: a funeral chapel spilling out onto the street. They came back every night. Nadia and Jean-François didn't approach, and stayed on the opposite side of the street. By 1 a.m. the crowd had dispersed. After three months the café reopened. They never went back.

After the quake of 13 November came the aftershocks. On Wednesday 18, Jean-François and Nadia finally went to the Paris Forensic Institute to see Lamia. Nadia agreed that a group of their daughter's friends could come along. The Paris Forensic Institute, or morgue, is a brick building beside the Seine on the Quai de la Rapée, where volunteers for the National Federation of Civil Protection greeted them with Thermoses of hot coffee. It was very cold. They were led into the office of a psychologist whose job it is to prepare families to see their loved one behind a pane of glass and for no more than three minutes to avoid 'thermal shock'. They might not recognise 'their' Lamia, she warned them, then took them into a darkened room. On a metal table behind the glass lay a body, covered to the chin with a white sheet, the head bandaged. Nadia and Jean-François stood in silence in front of this white form, fresh out of a cold room, that had been their little girl. Just as they were about to leave to sign the statement of recognition, shouts came from the door. One of Lamia's friends, one of the ones they hardly knew, was giving a roasting to the psychologist, repeating that there'd been a mix-up: the person under the sheet was not Lamia. At first incensed and unbending, the psychologist agreed to allow the young woman under the sheet to be examined. She had a tattoo on her ankle. Lamia did not. Nadia and Jean-François were filled with a wild hope that lasted until late that night, when they were all taken to the so-called ante-mortem cell of the École Militaire. There checks were done, cross-checks, DNA tests: Lamia had been mistaken for someone else, but she too was dead. Nadia had almost signed the statement saying she'd recognised her daughter when she'd seen someone else. If it hadn't been for the keen eyes of Lamia's friends she would have signed it – and probably never known any better. For Nadia these tender, precious friends are a gift from her daughter.

Over the next four years Jean-François Mondeguer worked tirelessly for the victims' association 13onze15, which he helped to found. He talked at lycées about terrorism and radicalisation, and so that people would not forget. He went to Brussels to attend the first trial of Salah Abdeslam and Sofien Ayari, who were charged with shooting at police officers during their arrest. But, Nadia says, sadness devoured him from the inside. On 29 February 2020 – a leap year day because Jean-François never did things like everyone else, Nadia says – he went to join his 'ladybird'. That's what he'd called Lamia when she was a little girl, and it's what he still called her even when she was thirty.

Together with Jean-François, Nadia had chosen to give birth to their three children at the Lilas Maternity Hospital, which promotes childbirth without pain. And yet Lamia left this world in the most violent of ways. It's so incomprehensible, says Nadia. To think that the people who killed her were her age. All of them between twenty-five and thirty. That they'd been taken by the hand on their way to school, just as she had taken Lamia by the hand.

They were little children, taken by the hand.

The silence in the room when she says this is as heavy as that of Lamia's friends on the evening of the 14th, in the living room on the Boulevard Voltaire.

Finally she says: 'Now, defence lawyers, do your job. Do it well. I mean it.'

In the pit

Clarisse: 'What I like at concerts is looking at people's faces. That night the faces were happy, everyone was in a fantastic mood. The energy was great.' Aurélie: 'The pit was full, maybe a thousand people, as soon as the firing started we got crushed against the barriers. I was hit by a bullet, I don't know which of the three shot it.' Lydia: 'I was facing the stage and could see the musicians. I saw how panicked they were, I saw them running backstage. At first I thought: some nutcase has come to shoot at the crowd.' Clarisse: 'I tried to believe: we're being taken hostage, if we do what they want it'll be okay. But no, after a couple of seconds it was clear that they were here to kill us and I thought this is totally crazy I'm going to die at the concert of some California rednecks that cost me 30 euros and 70 cents to get into.' Lydia: 'I tried to jump over one of the barriers but everyone was pushing and my leg got stuck, I asked if anyone had a knife so I could cut off my leg.' Amandine: 'What hurt the most was being trampled on.' Thibault: 'I threw my wife on the ground and jumped on top of her, everyone in the pit was lying down. After the first bursts of gunfire I saw a guy with a big build firing towards the ground. He moved forward calmly, a step or two, a shot, a step or two, a shot. He wasn't wearing a face mask. It was then, when I saw that his face was uncovered, that I realised we were all going to die.' Amandine: 'Right away I found myself lying in a pool of warm blood, I didn't understand how there could be so much of it so fast.' Gaëlle: 'I knew I'd been badly wounded when I tried to get the shoe of the guy lying on top of me out of my face. That was when I saw that my cheek had been ripped off and was hanging down beside my face. I put my right hand into my mouth to pull out my teeth so that I wouldn't choke on them, because otherwise I could gag and attract the terrorists' attention.' Thibault: 'I thought: this is it, here, now. This breath is my last. The only thought that eased my mind somewhat was that I didn't have any children.' Amandine: 'They'd turned on all the lights and were shooting people, I'd say with a certain relish.' Édith: 'They were very young, calm. At one point one of the killers' rifles must have got jammed and another helped him unjam it with a joke, like buddies at a shooting range.' Pierre-Sylvain: 'They stopped to reload and after that they slowed down: bullet by bullet, taking aim. A shout a shot, a sob a shot, a ringtone a shot.' Amandine: 'I didn't want to suffer any more, I thought okay I'm going to die at thirty-two, surrounded by people my age who like me have wonderful lives to live, killed by people who're getting a kick out of it.' Édith: 'A man stood up and said: "Stop it, what are you doing?" One of the killers shot him.' Helen: 'I heard him say, "There, that's for our brothers in Syria, if you don't like it talk to your President Hollande." I don't have the first idea what's going on in Syria, I'm here to have fun with Nick the love of my life and I ask Nick: "Have you been hit?" Yes, in the stomach, he's in pain, he's having trouble breathing so I breathe into his mouth and he dies.' Édith: 'He gave this little speech about Syria and it was like he couldn't give a shit, like a lesson you learn by rote but really don't care about, the only thing they cared about was shooting us. Pathetic.' Lydia: 'You move, you die. We pretend to be dead. Mobiles ring non-stop, with those distinctive iPhone jingles that still chill my blood six years later.' Pierre-Sylvain: 'One guy was shooting from the hip, then he lowered the barrel, put the butt to his shoulder and started firing downwards, each time at a specific target, killing us one by one. I was wounded. I looked over at Hélène. She had no nose and a hole in her right eye.' Édith: 'I managed to get up to the balcony, where a guy in the back row hid me under the seat.' Bruno: 'I was wearing a white T-shirt, I weighed 120 kg, a sitting duck. I lay in front of Édith, thinking maybe it would protect her.' Édith: 'I could hear the killing, curled up behind Bruno in the foetal position, waiting to die. I saw the door open at the other end of the balcony. The guy was three or four metres away, very calm, wearing white trainers.' Bruno: 'I thought to myself: hey, he's cool, he looks calm. Then he raises his gun and starts shooting down into the pit.' Aurélie: 'And then there was this horrifying explosion. I mean everything was already horrifying, I thought it couldn't get any worse, but this was one degree more horrifying. Like 9/11, I thought: the first plane, then after that the second plane.' Édith: 'There was a confetti of flesh everywhere. I remember thinking, there's no more milk in the fridge and I haven't paid my daughter's lunch fees.' Amandine: 'I saw feathers wafting down all around us, then I realised they were from his down jacket.' Gaëlle: 'I remember lying in a gooey bog, everywhere the smell of blood and gunpowder, and then the explosion, the bits of the suicide bomber raining down on us. In a hallucination I saw my son telling me: Mummy you have to get up, you have to get out of there.' Édith: 'A friend of Bruno's came over and said things were calming down, now was the time to escape. Bruno said I should come with them. I told him I couldn't move and he said: "Okay, I'll stay with you." And he stayed with me. A perfect stranger. Kudos, Bruno.' Amandine: 'I heard the police shouting: "Evacuate everyone who can walk on their own," and a man who was getting up saw my leg and said he was sorry but he couldn't help me.' Pierre-Sylvain: 'It was when I sat up that I saw the carnage. The blinding white light. The piles of bodies, a metre high, it reminded me of the pictures of the Jonestown massacre. The entire pit was covered with tangled bodies, impossible to tell the dead from the living. Add to that the pillars of smoke: an image impossible to unscramble, incomprehensible.' Aurélie: 'A young man helped me to get up and walk outside, then he went back into the Bataclan to help other survivors.' Édith: 'They got us to stand up and walk towards the exit in single file with our hands on our heads. They told us not to look, but I couldn't help looking. The sea of thick, black blood that kept getting bigger and bigger. All of these bodies that were drinking and dancing just an hour earlier. I saw the body of a young blonde woman, so beautiful, just that her limbs were all the wrong way round. The policeman said to me: "Keep moving, there's nothing more to be done here."' Coralie: 'I clutched my handbag, I was totally afraid of losing it because my health insurance card was in it and I was going to need it when I got to the hospital.' Gaëlle: 'Later I learned that the young surgeon who took me to the operating room in the hopes that they could save my face was a childhood friend: he didn't recognise me.' Édith: 'When I came out I saw Bruno pulling bits of flesh from the hair of a woman who was crying.' Bruno: 'There were three of us when we went in, four when we came out: all good.' Amandine: 'Later, just before he died, my father said to me: "You and me console other people for the misfortunes that befall us." I'd have preferred not to have to console you.'

In a tangle

Trampling, being trampled

The Bataclan can hold up to 1,498 people and it was packed that night. Nearly a thousand spectators in the pit alone. Standing, they were very close to one another. When they hurled themselves to the ground to avoid the first bursts of gunfire, they didn't fall next to each other but *on top of* each other. Voluntarily or involuntarily, those above protected those below. Several who were underneath described the warm, sticky liquid that oozed over them without their immediately understanding that it was blood. One survivor describes several layers of bodies. Everything was mixed up, in a tangle – the word 'tangled' comes up again and again. Another survivor says that when the killers stopped to reload she pushed on the floor to try to get up and escape. But the floor was soft: she wasn't pushing on the floor but on people, and they were no longer people but bodies. In the disorderly rush towards the exits, some of those fleeing necessarily trampled on others as they tried to get over them. Among the ones who got out alive, one woman said that for her the worst thing was being trampled. Others said that for them the worst thing was doing the trampling.

The mystery of goodness

The guilt that gnaws at most survivors is that they survived: why did others die, why am I alive? For some it's more personal. It has a face which haunts them. That of someone calling for help, someone they could perhaps have saved and didn't. Either because they had their hands full saving someone else, someone they loved, someone who came first, or because they put themselves first and saved their own skin. Those who acted that way cannot forgive themselves. Some say so, in poignant terms. The others forgive them, they say it's normal, only human. And they stress that many people did do the right thing, and often far more than that, going well beyond the dictates of morality. Stories of shipwrecks, catastrophes and run-for-your-life situations tend to reveal the worst in human nature. Cowardice, self-preservation, the bitter struggle for a place on the lifeboats of the *Titanic*. Here there's very little of all that. Barring the idea that the Bataclan survivors came up with a collective narrative of nobility and brotherhood – which is possible – one cannot help being impressed, session after session, by the recurrent examples of mutual help, solidarity and courage. By Bruno, who not only protects Édith, a complete stranger, with his heavy frame, but, when they get a chance to leave, says to her, 'Come on, let's go.' 'I can't move,' she replies, and he says calmly, 'Okay, I'll stay with you.' (Bruno works in the customer service department of the French railway company SNCF. He patiently listens to complaints, the only thing he lacks patience for is when a train is late and he's accused of 'taking passengers hostage'). By Clarisse, who with all the energy of James Bond in *GoldenEye* (her comparison) smashes a hole in a false ceiling to gain access to a hiding place, followed by about fifty people. Despite the panic the weakest are the first to be given a leg up, and no one says: okay, that's enough, we can't take everyone, it's full. By the commander of the BAC, or crime brigade, who, instead of waiting for reinforcements, disregards his seniority and decides on his own initiative to enter the Bataclan alone with his driver, knowing that they stand very little chance of coming back out alive. They only have small handguns against Kalashnikovs, yet the commander manages to shoot one of the terrorists who then blows himself up on the stage, and his act isn't only heroic but also effective: it stops the shooting, and the evacuations can begin. By the couples who stay together although one of them came out of the massacre disabled or disfigured.

Simone Weil

'Imaginary evil is romantic and varied; real evil is gloomy, monotonous, barren, boring. Imaginary good is boring; real good is always new, marvellous, intoxicating.'

We talk too much, and too complacently, about the

mystery of evil. Between being ready to die so as to kill or being ready to die so as to save: which is the biggest mystery?

The OAS

At the same time as V13, an interesting trial has been under way at the Paris Correctional Court. The defendants are six poor young white guys from Bouches-du-Rhône department in southern France. Logan Nisin, their leader, who was picked on at school for his spots and facial tics, went through a phase as a neo-Nazi (his email username was 'klausbraun', for Klaus Barbie and Eva Braun) before setting up the Facebook page 'Admirers of Anders Breivik' – the Norwegian racist who killed seventy-seven people in two attacks, most of the victims being young social democrats on an island summer camp. 'For me he wasn't a terrorist but a resistance fighter,' says Nisin. A believer in the theory of the 'great replacement' (of white Europeans by Muslim invaders), he created his own groupuscule called the OAS the day after 13 November. The initials stand for 'organisation of social armies' but are also a tribute to the French far-right paramilitary organisation during the Algerian War which bore the same initials, although one wonders, given his youth, how Nisin could even have heard of it. His website boasts posts like 'Arabs, blacks, dealers, migrants, scum, jihadists: want to waste one? Join us.' Or, even more succinctly: 'Now recruiting Arab-hunters.' He recruited half a dozen of them, over whom he exercised an authority that was all the more surprising in that he himself complained of his exceptional lack of charisma. One initiation rite he imposed on his new recruits was to 'pulverise' a randomly chosen Arab in the streets of Marseille. The action came to nothing, as the potential victim evaded their clutches without even suspecting the danger he'd been in. In spite of these less than auspicious beginnings, Nisin was thinking big and dreaming of emulating extremist models: Breivik, certainly, but also Dylann Roof (South Carolina, 2015, nine African Americans), Alexandre Bissonnette (Canada, 2017, six Muslims) and Brenton Tarrant (New Zealand, 2019, fifty-one Muslims). He tried his hand at fitting out a hunting rifle with a ten-round magazine, attempted to buy war weapons and triacetone triperoxide or TATP – the explosive used by today's jihadists – from members of the Serbian mafia, planned a large-scale massacre outside a mosque and the assassination of figures of the 'Islamo-left', among them far-left politician Jean-Luc Mélenchon, who testified at the trial although this project never stood a chance of actually being carried out. By and large, Nisin and his gang have planned a lot and achieved nothing. Their indisputable potential to cause harm has remained at the stage of bad intentions and hate posts. That did not prevent them from being arrested and indicted for 'criminal terrorist association'. The prosecutor who brought the case against them, playing on the fact that V13 was taking place at the same time, stressed the similarity between the OAS members' backgrounds and those of the jihadists they were fighting – 'two sides of the same coin' as she put it – and accentuated the still unrealised albeit extreme threat they posed. Their lawyers objected to her lumping the two trials together and pointed out that such cautionary sentencing is against the law. Logan Nisin got nine years. Two lessons can be learned from this trial. One: V13 brought to light dysfunctions in the intelligence services. People who were known to be extremists, who were trained in Syria and flagged with an S card as a serious threat to national security, were left to circulate freely because they hadn't committed any crimes, whereas public opinion no longer accepts such legalist procrastinating: we must strike *before* they do. Two: the terror threat is changing. The next major attack – because there is bound to be one – may well come not from the jihadist camp but from that of their emulators and sworn enemies: the white supremacists.

Eye contact

Bataclan, thirteenth day

When I came out of Roman Polanski's film *The Pianist*, I remember saying that I felt it had dragged on a bit. The friend I'd seen it with answered ironically: 'You know, life in the Warsaw Ghetto must have dragged on a bit too.' Today is the thirteenth day dedicated to the victims and survivors of the Bataclan, with five more to go. We've listened to nearly two hundred testimonies. Eighty additional plaintiffs have been announced in the past weeks. They're on the waiting list and will have to be heard from sooner or later. We can't take it any more. Too much suffering, too much horror. It's very unfair to the witnesses who were slotted in towards the end or testify late in the afternoon when attention is waning and half the hall has already left, but the fact is that the rooms of the Bataclan – the pit, the balconies, the passageways – the chronology of the killing and the escape routes taken by the survivors have been gone over so often that we no longer know how to absorb these words which, although they still tear us apart, no longer surprise us. The joyful atmosphere at the concert and the first shots that people mistook for firecrackers. The certainty that everyone was going to die, the instinct not to die. The smell of gunpowder and blood. The fact that the killers looked like they were having a good time. The tangled bodies, the cries of agony, the ringtones. The wounds the witnesses or others received, the discovery of just how much damage Kalashnikov bullets can make: holes in bodies the size of plates. Fearing for others even more than for yourself. Being led across the hall by police who tell you not to look but you can't help looking and you'll never forget what you saw. And then the difficult process of putting your life back together, the loss of a carefree attitude, the guilt at being alive. There isn't a single testimony that doesn't arouse terror and pity – the very emotions of tragedy. But what's inevitably becoming rarer is when someone says something new. Yet it happens.

The chosen one

When Guillaume approaches the stand, everyone feels that something is happening. This very handsome, serene, poised young man presents himself simply as 'the one the terrorist was holding at gunpoint onstage when the commander from the crime brigade arrived'. To recall the context: the three killers, whose names – Fouad Mohamed Aggad, Ismael Omar Mostefai, Samy Amimour – are now familiar, entered the Bataclan at 9.48 p.m. In ten minutes they'd killed ninety people and wounded some two hundred more. Then began another, much longer phase of the attack: the hostage-taking. Guillaume was in the pit when the first shots were fired, and tried to make his way between the wounded and the dead to an emergency exit. Two of the terrorists went up to the balcony from where they continued to shoot. The third, Samy Amimour, was on the stage. At that moment something happened, something with no parallel in the hundreds of testimonies we've heard so far. Everyone in the pit believed that their only chance of survival was to avoid any and all interaction with the terrorists. When one man stood up at the beginning and said, 'Why are you doing this? Stop!', he was immediately gunned down. You say a word, you're dead. You move, you're dead. The phone in your pocket rings, you're dead. You look at one of the killers, let's not even talk about it. This, notwithstanding, is what Guillaume says: 'I made eye contact with Samy Amimour and he gave me a sign that he wouldn't kill me, at least not for the moment. He said: "You, you're with us. Get up."' A question: what makes a guy who's killing people left and right suddenly choose one person out of all his potential victims and signal to him that he won't be killed? Someone to whom he says: 'You're with us'? 'Maybe if he didn't kill me it's because not many people made eye contact with him that night,' Guillaume says calmly. That, and the fact that the eleven hostages held on the balcony for the next two hours came out alive, seems to corroborate Emmanuel Levinas's idea that looking into someone's face is what forbids us from killing them (that said, the atrocious Islamic State beheading videos totally contradict this reassuring notion). Another explanation, which I'm advancing only very guardedly because it's so politically incorrect, is that there is something about Guillaume that *sets him apart* from others wherever he is, something that one is like it or not obliged to call aristocratic, and that it was this quality that earned him the privilege to be singled out in this way. 'He made me get up on the stage with him,' he goes on. 'It was once I was up there that I saw the carnage in the pit. The two others on the balcony yelled at me: "What're you're doing up there?" "It's okay," he told them, "he's with us." I said it too, hoping it would calm them down: "I'm with you."' At this point Guillaume had absolutely no idea how things would pan out. 'I was surprised by the terrorist's nonchalant, relaxed bearing. He was holding his rifle by the grip, at arm's length, like a toy, in a way that didn't seem . . . very professional.' Was the killer playing with him? Would this little game of cat and mouse end with a summary execution? At 9.59 p.m. two shadows which Guillaume immediately identified as 'benevolent' appear at the entrance. He was right, because these two shadows were the heroic crime brigade commander and his driver, who shot towards the stage with their small firearms and killed Samy Amimour. Guillaume had just enough time to leap into the pit and make a bolt for the emergency exit when the terrorist's suicide belt exploded, spraying the room with screws and bolts, feathers and human confetti. Silence. 'And afterwards?' asks the presiding judge. 'Afterwards,' replies Guillaume, 'is afterwards.' And in this afterwards, too, something exceptional happened. The commander of the crime brigade contacted Guillaume – and, as far as we know, only him. 'That meeting was decisive,' Guillaume says. 'I was face-to-face with someone who was trained to contend with delicate situations, and he helped me put a distance between acts and emotions.' In other words: after being the only one chosen by one of the killers, he was the only one chosen by the rescuer. After a few seconds of transfixed silence, Judge Périès asks Guillaume if he's receiving psychological support. In his dulcet voice, with a perfectly neutral tone that gives us all gooseflesh, he replies: 'No.' Renewed silence. End of testimony.

At home

According to a cruel aphorism, we all have strength enough to bear the misfortunes of others. This is true, yet even in the ranks of the observers – who when all is said and done have nothing more to do than listen and transcribe – we start feeling worse and worse. We sleep less and less well. We have nightmares, we grow irritable. And more and more often, once we're at home, without having seen it coming, we weep (and goodness knows, I'm not a big weeper).

Two fathers

The doors of dialogue

Everyone here projects themselves into the accounts we hear, but each in a different way. Often it's a question of age. I'm sixty-three, it's been a long time since I've been to a rock concert, my chances of having been at the Bataclan that night are as good as zero. My sons were twenty-eight and twenty-five in 2015, they could have been there. More than with the murdered young people themselves, I identify with their parents. With Nadia Mondeguer, whose daughter Lamia was killed at La Belle Équipe. With Georges Salines, whose daughter Lola was killed at the Bataclan. A lean, well-honed, retired doctor, Salines looks like a marathon runner. In fact he is a marathon runner. You get the feeling that if he's bald, it's so he can run faster. He comes to the trial every day, and over the past weeks he's simply become Georges to me, one of the few people I've befriended on this journey. We meet in the recesses in front of the only coffee machine, which is either taken by storm or out of order. And although the benches for the journalists are separated from those of the plaintiffs and the gendarmes do their best to ensure that everyone stays in their own section, we sometimes cheat and sit together, orange and green cords side by side, and comment on the hearing in hushed voices. The last time Georges saw his daughter was on the 13th at lunchtime. He'd planned to use the break to go swimming – he also swims – at the Butte-aux-Cailles swimming pool, near his office in the 13th arrondissement. Leaving the office, he bumped into Lola who was going to lunch with her colleague Manon. That wasn't surprising, as the two worked for Gründ Publishing House, whose office was a stone's throw from his own. They hugged and exchanged a few words. Lola said she'd see if she could come over for lunch at the weekend. She didn't mention that she was going to the Bataclan that night, only her brother knew. When the news broke they tried to reassure each other, not with magical thinking like Nadia Mondeguer but with statistics: 1,500 people were at the Bataclan, and the number of victims was being put in the dozens. Chances were vastly in favour of her coming out unscathed. At a pinch they were willing to concede that she could be injured, but not overly. For pity's sake, not overly. Georges later put the chance of falling victim to a terrorist attack in France at 2.2 in a million, far less than winning the jackpot. He never went back to the Butte-aux-Cailles swimming pool. In January 2016 he co-founded the association 13onze15 along with Jean-François Mondeguer. The two were very close friends until Mondeguer died; their daughters could have been friends as well. In memory of Lola he wrote a beautiful book of love and grief*, then he co-wrote another†, which shocked the group of victims because it's a dialogue with Azdyne Amimour, the father of Samy Amimour, the terrorist who blew himself up on the stage of the Bataclan. Already it's not the easiest thing in the world to admit that executioners' children are not responsible for the crimes of their fathers. As for their parents . . . Georges says that their pain must also be heard. He says that you can't fight barbarism with barbarism, and that what justifies a trial of this scope is its scrupulous respect for legal norms and principles. Georges advocates what's known as restorative justice. Developed together with the First Nations in North America, in South Africa after apartheid and in the wake of the Rwandan genocide, restorative justice involves fostering dialogue between victims and perpetrators, if both parties so wish: when the trials have ceased and with no talk of punishment, publicity or witnesses other than the prison guards, the only objective being for each person to tell their own truth and start putting their life back together, if possible. As an illustration Georges quotes Guillaume, the young man held at gunpoint by Samy Amimour on the Bataclan stage: 'Maybe if he didn't kill me it's because we made eye contact.' Eye contact, exchange, dialogue: listening to Georges, I remember what Salah Abdeslam

---

* Georges Salines, *L'Indicible de A à Z*, Seuil, 2016.
† Georges Salines and Azdyne Amimour, *Il nous reste les mots*, Robert Laffont, 2020.

said a few days earlier. Something like: 'Yes, it's a shame that there were Muslims among the victims. That's not what we wanted.' When the comment raised a hue and cry he said that people weren't trying hard enough to understand him, and that they should 'leave the doors of dialogue open'. For many, myself included, that took the biscuit. Coming from him, I found such a statement as embarrassing as when Adolf Eichmann said he'd like to find peace with his former enemies, or when Robert Ley, head of the Nazi Labour Front during World War II, was convinced that with a little goodwill and provided everyone acknowledged their wrongs, a 'conciliation committee' consisting of Jewish survivors and Nazi criminals could help everyone start over again on a new footing. Georges Salines is not of my opinion. He also wants to leave the doors of dialogue open. He's not only ready to exchange views with the father of one of his daughter's three killers, I think he'd be ready to talk with the killer himself if he weren't dead. And if Salah Abdeslam leaves the doors open to him, he'll take him up on it. At the end of his deposition Salines quotes French philosopher Vladimir Jankélévitch: 'Love for the wicked is not love for their wickedness, that would be a diabolical perversity. It is only love for the man himself, for the man who is the most difficult to love.'

The defence of hatred

Three days after Georges's testimony it's the turn of Patrick Jardin, a massive, graceless man who starts by congratulating the crime brigade commander for killing that 'scum' Samy Amimour and saying that people like Salah Abdeslam should be shot. Okay, the death penalty no longer exists, which is a pity, but at least these vermin will have to rot in prison for the rest of their lives before they burn in hell. Thirty-eight per cent of all Muslims in France approve of the killing of Samuel Paty – the history teacher beheaded in 2020 for showing his students cartoons depicting the Prophet Muhammad – he says, and it's time the authorities reacted in kind. 'People say I'm full of hatred, Your Honour, and it's true. I do hate, and what disgusts me the most are the parents of victims who don't. That guy who wrote a book with the father of one of the terrorists makes me puke.' Clearly, we who listen to Patrick Jardin cannot condemn this man who has lost his daughter. Nevertheless the flood of archaic fury that gushes from his mouth makes us uneasy. Learning to substitute law for retaliation, justice for revenge, is what we call civilisation. And Georges Salines is an eminently civilised man, someone I would like to emulate if such a misfortune befell me. Still, before we can overcome this archaic fury we must recognise that it exists – because it must exist, otherwise we wouldn't be human. Antoine Leiris, a young man whose wife was killed at the Bataclan, wrote a moving book, *Vous n'aurez pas ma haine* * (*You Will Not Have My Hate*), whose title has become a slogan. Although I admire the dignity of those who repeat this slogan in court, saying that they don't feel anger, that all they want is a fair trial, that to cry vengeance is to concede victory to the killers, first off it strikes me as too unanimous and virtuous to be entirely honest, and secondly I can't help thinking that they're far too quick in silencing the Patrick Jardin within themselves, and that if at least one time in every 250 we hear this sullen, unforgiving voice, it's a good thing. 'They say I'm on the far right, and maybe I am, I don't know, but even if I am on the far right, does that make my daughter any less dead?'

---

* Antoine Leiris, *Vous n'aurez pas ma haine*, Fayard, 2016.

The forgotten

The one hundred and thirty-first

Another Guillaume, more fragile than the one whose story so gripped us the other day, was also in the pit. When the shooting started he threw himself into the confused fray of tangled bodies on the ground. To his left a young woman was lying on her back. From the way she was looking up at the ceiling he knew she was dead. He was seized with a fit of uncontrollable trembling. Another young woman, on his right, took his hand. Over the crisp, deafening bursts of gunfire, he heard her whisper, close to his ear, 'It'll be okay ... it'll be okay ...' Then he walked, or crawled, through what he described to his parents as 'human mud'. With some others he took refuge in a dressing room where they hid for two hours, and from where he heard everything: the end of the shooting, the detonation of Samy Amimour's suicide belt, the assault, the cries of the wounded. When the survivors were evacuated he saw the pit. His father and brother found him numb with fright. In what follows he displays all the symptoms of post-traumatic stress: insomnia, nightmares, hypervigilance, panic attacks. The cries and whimpers from the pit haunt him and make him scream at night: they'll never stop. No more films, no more concerts, no more work, no more friends. His world is reduced to his room at his parents' place. Even there he's not safe. The outside invades the inside. The menace is deep within him. If he has trouble breathing, it's lung cancer. If he has pains in his stomach, it's cancer of the oesophagus. He's got every disease in the book. It'd be reassuring to know he has a definite physical illness. The only times he goes out are when he's driven to one hospital or another. X-rays, scans, MRIs, biopsies, they find nothing. Or rather, they do find something: hypochondriac delirium, melancholic depression. 'Melancholic' is almost graceful, it suggests that the person is sad, but that's not it at all. Guillaume's parents had no idea that psychological suffering could be so atrocious. They look on as their child sinks into a remote, desolate realm, from which there is no return. There's nothing they can do. They'd like to do something for him, the littlest thing, take him to the country for a weekend, make him something he likes to eat, but nothing helps. The last gesture that did him any good, the last one in this life that's devouring him from the inside, was when the young woman in the pit took his hand and said: 'It'll be okay . . . it'll be okay . . .' Still today his parents think about that unknown young woman. They wonder if she survived, they'd like to be able to thank her. In the autumn Guillaume is interned in a psychiatric ward, still convinced he's dying of cancer. He writes in his farewell letter: 'I have cancer of the oesophagus. The autopsy will confirm it.' On 19 November he's found hanged in his hospital room. Autopsy: no cancer. When people talk about the 130 victims of the attacks, says his father, they forget Guillaume, who took two years and six days to become the 131st. Thank you to those who do not forget him.

The nut

One emotion dispels another, one part of humanity displaces the next: the immense psychotherapy of the five weeks that are now coming to an end has had the beauty of a collective narrative and the cruelty of a casting call. Each witness came to the stand, read their prepared text, invited family and friends. It was a crucial moment in their life. To describe what was no doubt an equal amount of suffering, some found the right words and moved their listeners, others reeled off clichés and bored them. After half an hour it was time to move on to the next. The presiding judge would say: 'Thank you for your comments' (standard phrase), or, if the testimony was particularly powerful: 'Thank you for your moving words.' After which the speaker would head back up the aisle and sit down with the others. The Bataclan survivors are lucky in their misfortune: they're not alone. They're surrounded by others in the same situation. They go drinking together. They form a brotherhood. Since the start they're the ones who've attracted the

most attention, to the extent that it must be constantly
pointed out that the correct term is 'Paris attacks trial'
and not 'Bataclan trial'. Those who were on the terraces
complain that they're already second-class victims, but
the truly forgotten are those who were at the Stade de
France. They were only given one day, the first, and that
day now seems a very long way off. Before we move
on to a completely different phase of the trial – the questioning of the accused – I'm reminded of one of these
testimonies which has now all but faded into the past: that
of a graceful but very despondent young woman who
went with her TV crew to do a report on the fans at the
France–Germany match. The piece was already in the
can, but then in a second thought that cost her dearly
she said they should do some atmospheric shots outside
the stadium. It was there that she was knocked off her
feet by the blast. Let's recall that the three terrorists who
blew themselves up at the Stade de France were inept
enough not to do so inside the stadium – where it would
have been a massacre – but, as they got there too late to
go inside, outside where there wasn't a soul around and
where they only managed to kill a single person: which
is not much in view of the general tragedy, although
this one casualty is no less dead and his children no less
orphaned. Among the things an explosive belt projects
are nuts, bolts and screws, and one of the nuts embed-
ded itself in Marilyn's cheek. She could have been
disfigured, but she wasn't. One might be tempted to say
she got off lightly, but that's not the case: the cheerful

young woman she once was no longer exists. She talks about that young woman who danced, laughed and crossed Europe with a backpack, in whose skin she had loved to live, as if she were a ghost. She was fired from her new dream job. Her relationship fell apart. She returned to live with her parents, her life shrank. She's now unemployed, insomniac, afraid. She jumps at the slightest noise, she's always checking the emergency exits, and what's more nobody cares about what she's been through. So, you were a victim of the attacks. Were you at the Bataclan? No? On the terraces, then? No? At the Stade de France . . . Was there a bombing at the Stade de France? Oh, I had no idea. To make sure she remembers what everyone else forgets, Marilyn carries around with her a small plastic tube containing the 18 mm nut that was removed from her cheek. Standing before the court, she takes this tube from her bag and the nut from the tube, and says: 'I'll show it to you, but I'm keeping it.' Then she puts it back in her bag. Two hundred and fifty other testimonies will follow and obliterate her own, but I won't forget Marilyn as she walked away alone, so graceful and so sad, with her nut in its little tube.

The Accused

Three brothers

'Isn't this getting us too close to the facts?'

They call it the 'Paris attacks trial', the 'trial of terrorism', but that makes little sense: a trial is the trial of the accused, and that's what we're coming to now. For five weeks we've been listening to the atrocious, harrowing accounts of some 250 victims, and from time to time we've turned our gaze towards the box and wondered what could be going through the minds of the fourteen men in tracksuits who sit there behind or in front of the glass looking down at their trainers – waiting for it to be over with, I imagine. Then came their turn, for a week. One week isn't much, but we're still in the phase of the so-called 'personality' examinations. As for 'the facts' – including religion, considered as the first step towards the facts – they will be addressed starting January. Dedicating sessions to the defendants' personalities alone, dissociated from the acts that they've committed, is certainly odd, but this oddity is justified by the structure of the trial. It's so long, the material so abundant, that the decision was taken to divide it into chapters, like a novel: personality, radicalisation, Syria, preparation of the attacks, execution of the attacks, escape . . . Still, the ban on dealing with questions of religion or fact at this stage is a bit like the guy who starts psychoanalysis by saying: 'We can talk about anything you like, but I'd like to keep my private life to myself.' After one day of hearings, everyone has got used to the ban's arbitrary and at times comical nature. If talk comes round to the defendants' taste for travel, it's all right to say that he's been to Spain or England, but not to Turkey. No: that would get us too close to Syria, and so to the facts. One defendant, troubled by a question from one of the prosecutors, answers: 'Isn't this getting us too close to the facts?' Laughter in the courtroom, an indulgent smile from the presiding judge, the prosecutor beats a retreat: touché. So talk is limited to beforehand (childhood, brothers and sisters, studies, loves, professions where applicable), and afterwards (conduct in detention). And, at least as far as the 'beforehand' chapter goes, the defendants come across as good kids who're somewhat lost, moderately religious (even if this gets us very close to the facts, as their lawyers are quick to object), big smokers of weed (or dope, a nuance the presiding judge is slowly getting his head around), who go in and out of prison to a steady beat of petty offences. 'We weren't born with Kalashnikovs,' says Mohamed Abrini. And even Salah Abdeslam, the star of the trial who punctuated the first days with what can only be called inopportune remarks, now seems more like he's at the kind of job interview where you try to play down your youthful run-ins with the cops: being polite and smiling just the right amount. And everyone is happy that he's willing to play along, although in the end there's nothing he stands to gain one way or the other.

Molenbeek

Last year I did a piece in Brussels on a group of ten friends who opened a joint bank account. Each one deposits into it what he earns and withdraws what he needs, and against all odds, it works. The initiators of this experiment, almost all of them artists, transformed a former biscuit factory in Molenbeek – a district in the centre of Brussels with the unpleasant reputation of being the centre of European jihadism – into a co-working space. As good middle-class lefties – and I'm not one to throw stones – they'd like to describe Molen-beek as a multicultural neighbourhood. But even they have to admit that it's almost totally monocultural – ninety-five per cent of its inhabitants are Muslim, the women wear the niqab, and the rare attempts at creating a cultural mix in the form of convivial cafés or alternative day-care centres meet with little success. It is not, however, a dangerous neighbourhood for *kuffar* – as my new friends and I, as non-believers, are called in Arabic. They're ignored, but not threatened in any way. When the group took me to see the building where Salah Abdeslam was arrested – the high point of the 'jihad tour' that curious visitors are taken on – in a street very close to theirs, I did not suspect that a year later I'd find myself in a large white wooden box a few metres from the self-same Salah Abdeslam, trying day after day to understand who he is, where he comes from, and what's going on in his head. Nor did I suspect that I'd be listening with such keen interest to the Belgian investigating judge Isabelle Panou – a truculent woman who tells the V13 court how Molenbeek became what it is, and how radical Islam became rooted in Belgium. In 1969, Panou explains, in an effort to oversee its immigrant population, most of whom were Moroccan, the Belgian government got the idea of entrusting the management of the Muslim faith to a 'neutral' power that had the funds to finance it: Saudi Arabia. Not a good idea. Under the authority of this petroleum monarchy which was both monstrously rich and monstrously backward, Belgium – and in particular Molenbeek – became a breeding ground for Islamists where, in the next generation, seven of the defendants in the box and three dead members of the commando grew up. In this village measuring six square kilometres, with twice the population density and three times the unemployment of the rest of Brussels, they lived within walking distance of each other – as shown by the little blue pins indicating their homes on the map that Judge Panou has had projected onto the screen. They grew up together, went to school together, got into trouble together, all of which was relatively harmless until a big, dark and alluring bit of trouble came along in 2012 and turned their lives upside down.

Russian roulette

Because their last names come one after the other in the alphabet, Salah Abdeslam and Mohamed Abrini sit next to each other in the box and spend a lot of time talking. From time to time the presiding judge has to call them to order. Abdelhamid Abaaoud, the leader of the commando, isn't there with them because he died four days after the attacks, in the squat where he'd holed up in the northern Parisian suburb of Saint-Denis. The three of them were childhood friends: 'three brothers'. Abdeslam and Abrini come from homes that Abrini defines as 'not rich but not poor either'. They're not welfare cases, none of the defendants are, but the Abaaoud family is considerably better off. While Abdeslam's father – who like most of the people in Molenbeek arrived from Morocco in the early 1970s – is a tram driver for the Brussels Transport Company, Abaaoud's father owns not one but *several* clothing shops: he's looked up to in the community, and enrols his son Abdelhamid in one of the best Catholic schools in Brussels. Salah Abdeslam describes his family as loving and close-knit, 'people who've never caused anyone any trouble', and himself as a nice, quiet guy, good enough at school to graduate with a technological baccalaureate. Tall and slim, he likes to dress well, he's quick-witted and even elegant in a casual sort of way. Before he's twenty he has a girlfriend, Yasmina, who's said to be pretty and well mannered. She's listed as a witness in the trial but it's not known if she'll come, no one really believes she will. All in all Salah Abdeslam doesn't cut such a bad figure. With Mohamed Abrini things are more complicated: less talented, less of a smooth talker, with a boxer's shoulders and a weasel's face, he sums up his life in the gloomy formula: 'bad at school, bad at sports, bad full stop'. And, when the presiding judge points out that his 'brother' managed to succeed in life, he answers: 'If you take everyone who's failed in Molenbeek and everyone who's succeeded, it's 80 to 20. A whole lot fail, not too many succeed, I'm in the first group.' Initially an apprentice baker (hence the nickname 'Brioche'), he soon turns to petty crime, in particular cracking safes in garages (hence the nickname 'Brink's'). In a way Abrini is Abdeslam's underling: the burly guy who's slow on the uptake, not much to look at and hard to get into clubs – because all three like to go clubbing. Abdelhamid Abaaoud plays the role of evil genie in the lives of the other two. Small and slight, unattractive, with a sardonic grin, he's a disturbing clown subject to sudden mood swings, changing from one minute to the next like the petty gangsters in Scorsese films: you can be talking normally and without warning he'll grab you by the hair and slam your head into a pan of hot oil. With his father's money, Abaaoud drives a four-by-four, goes on weekend jaunts to Marrakech, and gambles for high stakes at the casino where the three play 'poker, blackjack and Russian roulette', says Abrini. The presiding judge raises an eyebrow:

'Russian roulette?' 'Well, roulette,' concedes Abrini, who doesn't seem to grasp the implications of his slip. Abdeslam and Abrini have trouble keeping up with their high-rolling friend. Abdeslam goes to work for the Brussels Transport Company thanks to his father, who pulled some strings, but it depresses him. He can't see himself fixing trams his whole life for a salary that doesn't even pay for a half-decent weekend. It's not for him. Yasmina, his fiancée, worries: she doesn't like these weekends where of course she's not invited and where her fiancé drinks, gambles and hits on *kafir* bimbos. She's a good Muslim from a good family – it goes without saying that she'll be a virgin bride. She's leery of Abaaoud's sway over Salah, and she's right to be. In 2010 the two attempt a burglary, which backfires. A year's suspended sentence of which they have to serve a month. Not a lot, but enough to make Abdeslam no longer welcome at Yasmina's parents' house and get him fired from the Transport Company, so he goes from one under-the-table temp job to the next, and finally starts hanging out at the café run by his brother Brahim, Les Béguines. Brahim is his elder brother, less charming, more chunky. Everyone agrees that he had a big mouth and brutal manners, and that around him you watched your step. Les Béguines is a seedy bar no *kafir* would ever think of entering, where a small group of dealers and heavy users, most often both, like Mohammed Amri, Hamza Attou and Ali Oulkadi, the minor defendants in the trial, hang out in a thick cloud of dope smoke. Sitting around with this society of losers who spend their time stewing in their own juices, Salah Abdeslam feels cut off from the vibrant life he led in Abaaoud's company. But Abaaoud has disappeared because his father hit on an idea – one as bad as the Belgian government's plan to hand over the keys of its mosques to Wahhabi imams from Saudi Arabia. Sincerely believing he was putting the turbulent young man back on track, he sent him to study for a year at a Quranic school in Cairo, in the shadow of the Al-Azhar Mosque – the heart of Sunni Islam. After leaving Brussels as a secular thug, Abaaoud returned as a Salafist thug. But here we leave the field of the personality and start to touch on the facts, so I won't get ahead of myself.

First gambits

The rules of the game

Salah Abdeslam played chess while he was in prison, but he gave it up when he discovered that it's forbidden by the Quran. All of us on the press benches snatch up our phones to check if it's true: it's not. The Prophet only forbids games of chance, which chess most definitely is not. It was the Grand Mufti of Saudi Arabia who declared such games *haram*, on the grounds that they waste time and money and cause hatred between the players. I wouldn't call it hatred, but what we see taking place during these first interrogations is very much like the opening gambits of a chess game, when the players push their pawns with a specific strategy in mind. Let me summarise the rules. Each defendant is first questioned by the presiding judge and assistant magistrates, who are careful to remain neutral and stick to the facts. Then come the public prosecutors, who represent the interests of society. It's on behalf of society and not this or that victim that they question the accused, construct their arguments and deliver their closing speeches. Whereas the presiding judge is aided by four female magistrates, the chief public prosecutor, a woman, is seconded by two men: another, younger, face of justice. None of the public prosecutors is over forty, and all three are clearly very good. I met the chief prosecutor, Camille Hennetier, in the spring when I came to meet the national counter-terrorism prosecution service. Together with her colleague François Molins, she was the first prosecutor to enter the Bataclan, she's been handling this monstrous case day and night for six years, and right from the start I've been struck by the measured, precise nature of her remarks. Dark-haired and elegant in bearing, she is clear without being cold, and when she stands up to speak the hall falls silent (okay, I'm a fan, but not the only one). After the public prosecutors come the plaintiffs' counsel, and here things are more chaotic. There are 350 of them, not all present at the same time of course. Many never come at all, or very rarely. Twenty or perhaps thirty are there all the time. They're here to represent their clients and establish the harm suffered by them – as opposed to the harm inflicted on society as a whole. But their questions often dovetail with those of the public prosecutors, with the result that the distinction between them is not always entirely clear. Some of them I like a lot: Sylvie Topaloff, whose beautiful, hoarse voice resounds with anger and intelligence, and Jean-Marc Delas, a nonchalant beanpole who makes a point of speaking as little as possible, pleading as little as possible, and basically disturbing the goings-on as little as possible: a Taoist lawyer and one of my most steadfast buddies during the recesses. Finally it's the turn of the defence lawyers – the unbreakable rule of French legal procedure being that the defence has the last word. They are fewer in number: each defendant generally has two, given the difficulty of getting one's head around such a huge dossier. So in all there are around thirty of them in front of the box, and they're obliged to be present at all times. Whether the questions are asked by the court, the prosecution, the plaintiffs' lawyers or the defence, everyone can ask to speak at any time: that's the twin principle of contradictory and orality of debates. There you go, that's more or less it.

Terrorist offenders, or offenders tout court

Since those who did the killing are all dead, the defendants are by definition only accomplices; however, their degrees of complicity vary substantially. Right at the top of the chain is Salah Abdeslam, who was part of the commando and should have blown himself up like his brother Brahim. He alone will be able to say whether if he didn't it was because his belt was defective, because he was afraid, or because at the last minute he thought that what he was about to do was not at all nice. If established, this last moral scruple could work in his favour, but it won't prevent him from spending if not the rest of his life then at least long, long years behind bars. Those in the middle of the chain don't come from Molenbeek but from Syria, they didn't participate directly in the attacks but they could have or should have, and they're said to be seasoned fighters of the Islamic State: Osama Krayem, Sofien Ayari, Muhammad Usman, Adel Haddadi. They can also reckon with stiff sentences. Finally, at the bottom of the chain come the petty offenders, or even non-offenders: Mohammed Amri, Hamza Attou, Ali Oulkadi, Yassine Atar, Farid Kharkhach, whose lawyers have a reasonable chance of proving that yes, they played a part in the attack, but by chance and without really knowing what they were doing. This is what it all comes down to: who knew what? Did the person who rented a car or flat think he was helping with a job that wasn't entirely above-board, or did he knowingly lend a hand in the massacre of 131 people? Legally speaking, is what he did criminal association, or criminal terrorist association? In the first case it's not too serious: as he's been in prison for six years he could even go free. In the second, whatever happens, he'll get the max.

Kamikaze

In these first thrusts and parries between the prosecutors, who seek a conviction for criminal terrorist association, and the defence lawyers who say their clients were simply aiding and abetting a criminal offence, some things escape us. For example, there was a long argument about whether the defendant Yassine Atar was nicknamed Yass. The prosecutors, having read all the text messages on his phone, found quite a few in which he's addressed as Yass. His lawyers counter that there are a lot more in which he's not. I have a hard time seeing why they're fighting tooth and nail on this until Violette Lazard, my colleague at *L'Obs*, explains: in a computer used by the terrorist cell that was found in a rubbish bin in Brussels just after the bombings there on 22 March 2016, there are numerous references to a certain Yass, and this apparently innocent nickname is in fact the crux of the matter, the point that will tip Yassine Atar's fate one way or the other. A little later the focus is on Mohammed Amri, who drove to Paris with Hamza Attou on the night of the attacks to pick up Salah Abdeslam and bring him back to Brussels. His lawyers, Negar Haeri and Xavier Nogueras, push their pawns in the hope of demonstrating that their client went there thinking he was getting his friend out of a drug or car deal gone sour, certainly not a terrorist attack, and that what kept him from denouncing Abdeslam when he realised what he'd done was not jihadist solidarity but simply the moral code of the Molenbeek thugs: you don't rat on a brother, no matter what he's done. With a series of precise, well-turned questions, Haeri establishes that her client 1) is obliging and loyal, someone you can count on; 2) likes to drive; and 3) is always stoned at the wheel because the first thing he does when he wakes up in the morning is smoke a joint – which of course impairs his judgement. Nogueras then takes over and pushes another pawn by asking his client if, in addition to being obliging, loyal and always driving high, he likes to listen to music while he drives. You can see where he's heading: fundamentalist Muslims have the right to play chess, contrary to what Abdeslam believes, but not to listen to music. 'Sure,' Amri nods, 'I listen to music.' 'What kind of music?' 'Rap.' 'What songs?' Nogueras prods, to hammer home to all those present that yes, his client really does listen to music. 'Uh,' Amri says candidly, '"Kamikaze".'

The game has only just begun.

Hollande's day in court

A dispute

Much excitement on this Wednesday 13 November: former president François Hollande is to be heard. All of the tourist journalists who came on the first day and were no longer there on the second are back – forcing us to squeeze together again on the benches where we've made ourselves comfortable. As a crowd-warmer before the star arrives there's a bizarre little debate – bizarre because it's both completely superfluous and excellently argued – about whether the former president's testimony has a place in the trial. What light could his being called to the stand shed on the facts, the personality or the morality of the accused (the triple criteria, I learn, required by Article 331 of the French Code of Criminal Procedure to justify such an appearance)? Since those who were inside the Stade de France – where nothing happened – have been refused the status of plaintiffs, why make such a fuss about Hollande, who was also there, sure, but at whom no one, as far as is known, so much as took a shot? Why the special treatment? Because he was the president of France at the time of the attacks? Obviously, the answer is yes: because he was the

99

president of France. And because it was him, by name, that the terrorists mentioned in their attacks. In the terrible audio tape of the Bataclan attack, we heard them say: 'You can thank your president François Hollande. If we kill you it's his fault. He started this when he bombed our wives and children.' Despite the symbolism of this non-issue raised by some of the defence lawyers to trigger a few tweets, the popular wisdom is to conclude with Camille Hennetier: the appropriateness of his testimony may be judged once he's been heard – and now that Hollande's here we're not about to ask him to turn around and go home.

A pebble in his shoe

While waiting for the former president to arrive we take bets: will the hearings be disrupted? Will Salah Abdeslam come out of his box, as he did at the beginning of the trial and as he's completely stopped doing since then? My friend Jean-Marc Delas, the Taoist lawyer, sees the following scenario: as Hollande approaches the stand, even before he has a chance to open his mouth, Abdeslam stands up and points at him, yelling: 'He's the one who stands accused! He should be in this box!' And let's admit: as attached as we are to calm debate, we can't help hoping something like that will happen. But nothing does. Or rather, one thing does: there's a confused and belated protest by Abdeslam, whom Jean-Louis Périès immediately cuts off because presidents – in this case of the court and of the country – have to have each other's back. Hollande is dignified, articulate, a little stiff but not without a dose of humour: in short himself. The plaintiffs' lawyers pose respectful and for the most part futile questions, to which he replies in essence that if he had to do it all over again he'd do everything the same way. The only one who tries to challenge him is Abdeslam's feisty young lawyer Olivia Ronen. This in a nutshell is her argument. According to the terrorists, their attacks are a legitimate response to the state terrorism practised by France first in Iraq and then in Syria. You massacre innocent people in our country, we massacre innocent people in yours. An eye for an eye, a tooth for a tooth – we didn't start it, you did. According to the French state, not only would such a response be inadmissible, but the whole argument doesn't hold water because the Islamic State threatened France *before*, and not after, the first strikes in Iraq. In Hollande's words: we were attacked for what we *are* – the country of freedom – not for what we've done. Everyone seems to agree, yet this is precisely what Ronen contests. 'One moment, Mr President,' she says, 'let's examine the order of events. On 29 June 2014, from the minaret of the Mosul Grand Mosque, Abu Mohammad al-Adnani, spokesperson for the Islamic State, proclaims the caliphate. On that we can agree?' Hollande can't disagree, it's an objective fact, nevertheless he wonders where this is leading. 'On 21 September 2014, the same al-Adnani solemnly calls for the West, the Americans, and above all the "evil, dirty French" to be punished. And when do the first French strikes in Iraq take place?' 'Uh,' answers Hollande, who smells a trap, 'at the end of September . . .' (So after al-Adnani's threats.) 'No,' says Ronen, 'on 19 September.' (So before.) The upshot? France strikes the Islamic State, and two days later the Islamic State announces that it will strike France. Strictly speaking then, based on the chronology of events, the terrorists are right: we, France, declared war on the peace-ful citizens of the Islamic State. It's a detail, we quickly move on to something else, but it strikes me that Ronen is fighting bravely with the few cartridges at her disposal, and I wonder if this detail, this little pebble in Hollande's shoe, isn't also a pebble on the path to a defence of rup-ture, as worked out and brilliantly applied by Jacques Vergès in his defence of Klaus Barbie exactly thirty-five years ago. I've already brought it up, chances are I'll do it again: V13 often brings to mind the Barbie trial. In Lyon, as today in Paris, the staging was spectacular. The front lobby of the Rhône Assize Court was transformed into a courtroom capable of holding seven hundred people, the judges' bench and witness box were raised, and everything was filmed. It was to be an exemplary, his-toric tribunal that put Nazism, the Occupation, and torture on trial. Except that . . . Except that there was Vergès, who put all his talent into eking out every nuance of an argument similar to the one Abdeslam is now making: your justice is worthless and I do not recognise it. Yes, the Gestapo tortured in France, but France tortured in Algeria and nobody thinks of putting it on trial. Every time you bring up Nazism I'll counter with colonialism. And don't tell me that has nothing to do with it because it does. Put your own house in order first.

Terror's Advocate

This is the title of Barbet Schroeder's wonderful documentary on Vergès – a fiery character who started out as a courageous Third World activist before becoming, via the Palestinian cause, the defender of all of the terrorists of the 1970s, several bloodthirsty – but Marxist – dictators and, the crowning achievement of his career, a Nazi butcher. Ensconced in the golden gloom of his office in front of his Khmer statuettes – given to him, for all anyone knows, by Pol Pot – he smiles like the Cheshire Cat and has an unctuous, sardonic voice: the dream villain for a James Bond film. Barbet Schroeder asks him what he remembers about the Barbie trial. He revels in the question, turns the adjective over in his mouth before letting it drop: 'It was euphoric!' He takes a drag on his cigar, delighted with himself, and continues: 'There were forty lawyers for the plaintiffs on one side, and only me on the other. Each of them was worth one-fortieth of me. Before the trial Roland Dumas, who was later foreign minister under Mitterrand, told me he'd been asked to represent an association of members of the Resistance. "What do you think?" he asked. I replied: "I don't recommend it. Don't think I'm afraid of you, I'm not. It's just that there are going to be forty of you bravehearts singing the same song and feigning the same emotions that you don't feel: human dignity . . . the duty of remembrance . . . never again . . . If they're good actors, the first three will have some success. But starting with the fourth, people will say: 'Enough! Enough!'" Dumas did it anyway, but let me ask you: can you tell me the name of a single one of those forty tenors across from me? A trial is a magical place, it's a box of surprises. Quavering voices declared "Never again" a hundred times, but in fact everyone was only thinking one thing: what is that bastard Vergès going to come up with today? That amuses me, thrills me, but it's not just that. I can't stand it when people are humiliated. I can't stand it when a single person, even if he's the last scum on earth, is harassed by a lynch mob. Someone once asked me: "Would you have defended Hitler?"' Again, the Cheshire Cat smile. 'I replied: "I'd even defend Bush."'

'Individuals who came from nowhere'

The gendarmes' point of view

Entering the Palais de Justice during V13 is like taking a plane: you show your badge and ID at two successive checkpoints, empty your bag and pockets and go through metal detectors, and if you have a bottle of water you have to take a sip to prove it's not TATP – the explosive liquid that jihadists call the 'mother of Satan'. The gendarmes who carry out these checks are both thorough and remarkably friendly. They take all the precautions they've been instructed to take, but show with a benign smile that they're not targeting *us*. Who, *us*? We, the lawyers, journalists and plaintiffs, whom nobody could mistake for terrorists. As trained at being suspicious as they may be, the gendarmes are clearly not on high alert when they see, approaching with a badge around his neck, a guy like me – a white male in his sixties, visibly at ease, who looks every bit the part of a good citizen with nothing at all to reproach himself for, someone who's so unafraid of being asked to show his ticket in the metro that there's not the slightest chance he'll ever be asked. Then who would be suspicious from the gendarmes' point of view? Who would immediately put them on the alert? The answer is shameful but certain: an Arab. A 'North African type', as the police reports say: young, wearing tracksuit bottoms and a hoodie, doubly so if he's got a full beard. There's no one like that here with us. The only people like that we see in this trial are in the box.

The expert's point of view

It's the logic of 'us and them' in its purest form. Us: the peaceful democrats, honest souls on whom V13 acts as a powerful machine for creating community, ties and a sense of identity. We look alike, understand each other, recognise one another. Across from us: them. Those who do not look like us, whom we don't know or understand. The only vague thing we think we know about these opaque young men – 'these individuals who came from nowhere, sending weak signals', as the public prosecutor François Molins described them – is that they want us dead, and that they prefer death to life, even for themselves. So we're glad that experts and researchers will take the stand to explain to us who these people are and what's going through their minds. The first is Hugo Micheron. He's an Arabist, a Princeton professor, thirty-three years old, good-looking, nice suit, and so obviously on the right side of society that one wonders how he was able to gain the trust of the hundred or so jihadists he spent five years interviewing – in the neighbourhoods where they grew up, in Syria where they went, in the prisons where they're now incarcerated. But he gained it, and I entirely agree with Mathieu Delahousse, my colleague at *L'Obs*, who'd already recommended his book *Le Jihadisme français* * to me, and who said straight out at the end of the hearing that the guy had 'shed light in the darkness'. One of the many ideas that struck me in his presentation is that for us a jihadist is an enigma, a threat, but also a victim, the sick and cruel product of a sick and cruel society. To end up where he is, we think, he must have been rejected, humiliated, marginalised by a pitiless socio-economic system, with no other options than crime or a religion gone mad. Micheron does not deny that all of that is true, or that some of the jihadists he's met can be considered victims in that sense – which comes down to a class struggle. But what must never be forgotten, he stresses, is that from their point of view they don't see themselves as victims or welfare cases. On the contrary, they see themselves as heroes, on the vanguard of a grand and irresistible movement of global conquest. The true victims, in their eyes, are the pitiful 'moderate' Muslims, the estranged collaborators who want to believe that Islam is compatible with the values of the corrupt society in which they live. They're the *kuffar* who claim – like me and, I imagine, like you – to be open and tolerant,

---

* Hugo Micheron, *Le Jihadisme français*, Gallimard, 2020.

whereas in the jihadists' view the only respectable *kuffar* are the far-right identitarians who couldn't agree more with them that their civilisations are radically incompatible. There is a jihadist pride, a jihadist confidence, and that explains why the de-radicalisation programmes work so badly. It's as if the Roman Empire had launched de-Christianisation programmes in the first century: it would only have confirmed the candidates for martyrdom in their acts. Once you've committed your life to a just and glorious struggle, one that immerses your very soul and in which victory is assured on earth as in heaven, why go over to the losers' side?

In al-Sham

Perhaps we could, or should, go back in time. To the Hijrah, the birthing act of Islam when the Prophet left Medina for Mecca, or to the end of the Ottoman Empire. But as he only has four hours at his disposal, Micheron starts his historical presentation in December 2010, when a Tunisian fruit merchant, Mohamed Bouazizi, sets himself on fire because he's had enough of the omnipresent misery and oppression. Very quickly, the fire spreads throughout the country and to the neighbouring states, and becomes what's known as the Arab Spring. Crowds roaring in anger, crowds shouting in triumph, dictators on the run: Ben Ali in Tunisia, Mubarak in Egypt, Gaddafi in Libya. Immense hope: what if, one day, finally, the Arab world can escape the sinister treadmill of corrupt colonels and bloodthirsty beards that culminated in the Algeria of the 1990s? The uprising reaches Syria, but there the dictator has more staying power. Bashar al-Assad's repression is horrific. Torture, peaceful demonstrations put down with machine-gun fire, dead bodies in the streets. Deserting officers create the FSA, or Free Syrian Army, with the aim of overthrowing the regime. It's the start of a civil war that will leave 500,000 dead and force half the country's population to flee. It's also the start of what Micheron terms the jihadisation of the rebellion. Mobilised across Europe over the internet, young radical Muslims with a thirst for adventure understand that 'some crazy stuff is going down in Syria'. A generation ago they'd have gone to Afghanistan to support the mujahideen, now they descend on a country they no longer call Syria but al-Sham. A land of fire and blood, but also a promised land, heralded by the most ancient Muslim prophecies. A land where, once Bashar is defeated, everyone will live as the Prophet's companions lived in the first days of Islam. A land where the most rigorous sharia law will apply: thieves' hands will be cut off, adulteresses will be stoned. God's reign on earth, joy in heaven. Some come to al-Sham to fight because they like to fight, others because they sincerely want to help build a country, a society, a utopia – like the Jews in Israel, one young jihadist says quietly. It's into this cauldron that Abdelhamid Abaaoud plunges in the spring of 2013. You remember: the little thug-cum-poser from Molenbeek who's at the centre of this story, the boyhood friend of the Abdeslam brothers, whose father sent him to a Quranic school in Cairo to straighten him out? Instead of settling down and taking over the family's shops, he comes back 'radicalised', as people were starting to say, and then off he goes again to where the 'crazy stuff' is going down. Between the warriors and the builders his choice is quickly made, and he just as quickly finds his place in the subcategory of psychopathic warriors. He does his apprenticeship at al-Ayoun eye surgery hospital in Aleppo, whose cellars hold Western hostages. There he rubs shoulders with a certain Mehdi Nemmouche, who in his own words is a 'criminal turned Islamic ethnic cleanser', and who will go on to attack the Jewish Museum in Brussels in May 2014. The conflict between Bashar's army, the Free Syrian Army and al-Qaeda – initially the dominant jihadist organisation – is becoming increasingly hard to follow. What with my enemy's enemy being my friend and my enemy's friend being my enemy, etc., one tends to get lost, especially when al-Qaeda is supplanted on the ground by the Islamic State, founded in the summer of 2013 by Abu Bakr al-Baghdadi. A year later, on 29 June 2014, its spokesperson, Abu Mohammad al-Adnani, announces the restoration of the caliphate from the Mosul Grand Mosque. This is a crazy proclamation from all points of view, Micheron relates.

The previous caliphate was the Ottoman Empire, abolished by Mustafa Kemal Atatürk in 1924, exactly ninety years earlier. Those ninety years were ninety years of misfortune for the Arabs, who were humiliated and relegated to a filthy suburb of the world. In the countries where misery drove them to seek their fortunes they were reduced to the miserable condition of immigrant workers: furtive, sexually frustrated shadows. In France, the first generation dwelt in the poor conditions of Sonacotra – or National Agency for the Construction of Housing for Workers – hostels, while the second, still not really integrated and torn between contempt and pity for their poor parents, are doomed to spend their time propping up the walls of their housing estates, dealing dope and trashing the lifts. Now, however, the story goes, the ninety years of misfortune are over. The Arabs, who for five centuries had the grandest empire in the world, are reclaiming their glorious place in history. Cries of joy broke out when the Twin Towers collapsed. Now the caliphate exists. For the first time, a terrorist organisation rules over a territory the size of France, an organisation which everyone may join. Which everyone *must* join, so as to submit the entire planet to Quranic law as ordered by the Prophet. Al-Qaeda was elitist in its recruitment, giving preference to engineers, intellectuals, theologians. The Islamic State welcomes everyone under its black flag: spotty teenagers, idealists, clowns and fools, raving lunatics, everyone is welcome, everyone is promised an El Dorado with housing, women, weapons, hostages to torture for those who like it, and many like it. Appointed emir of the foreigners' brigade, 'a group of buddies who get a kick out of massacring and beheading as if they were at some kind of gruesome holiday camp' (as one of their wives describes them), the young Abaaoud blossoms and attains worldwide jihadist fame thanks to a video found by soldiers of the Free Syrian Army on an abandoned phone sold to journalists at the French television station BFM TV. Sitting behind the wheel of a four-by-four, he turns to the camera and says with a smirk: 'Before, we used to haul jet skis, quads, motocross bikes or trailers full of holiday gifts. Now we haul *kuffar*.' He pulls away, and behind the truck we see metal cables dragging seven or eight bodies in the dust. Cut, and there he is again, still grinning, playing football with a severed head. 'Shoot, brother,' he cries, 'kill the *kuffar*, look at this one with the head of a Smurf!' Sporting a pakol hat worn by the Afghan mujahideen, he beams, happy with his joke. Electrified by such videos, all sorts of people who not so long ago knew nothing about the jihad now have nothing better to do than leave for al-Sham. Those who read the fine print are chilled to discover at the bottom of their arrival forms: 'Date and place of death.' Many will be killed, without even knowing whether it's by Syrian loyalists, rebels or their own leaders. The Islamic State, says Micheron, is the only army in the world that shows utter disregard for the lives of its soldiers. Who cares if they die: as martyrs they'll go straight to paradise. If they want to leave, on the other hand, it's more complicated. Many who were thrilled to arrive now find themselves trapped. You can get in, but you can't get out. Micheron spells all this out in considerable detail, I'll be brief. The years 2015–16, with the huge wave of attacks in Europe, are the zenith of the Islamic State. Then the coalition bombing intensifies and the top jihadist leaders are killed one after the next. The caliphate collapses in 2017. Vladimir Putin announces the end of the war in 2018. From 2019 on, the problem is to bring the French jihadists still in the area, and in particular their wives and children, back to France. Another chapter.

In prison

In 2017, Europe emerged from the paroxysmal period of attacks as suddenly as it entered it in 2015. One would like to believe that this archaic, artisanal form of barbarism had been relegated to the past. But in the history of jihadism, Micheron explains, there are periods of retreat and periods of expansion. Diastolic and systolic moments, as in any story, starting with that of the Prophet who preached secretly in the shadows of Mecca to a few companions, before becoming a public figure in Medina and launching his prodigious series of military conquests. What brought about the downfall of the Islamic State, according to jihadist thinkers – and there are some – was haste. It was believing that the Medina phase had come although they were still in the Mecca phase. A small, heroic vanguard was ready, but not the mass of believers – not even the ten per cent who could have tipped the scales. A tactical retreat became necessary, a base was needed, and that base is prison. Prison is the laboratory of jihadism in the 2020s. In a population that is half Muslim, the arrival of a hundred or so 'returnees', who benefit from the prestige of the Syrian adventure, has had a devastating effect. At first they were dispersed in various detention centres, where their influence was so great that all of the common-law prisoners at Fleury-Mérogis Prison howled with joy for hours when they heard about the Nice truck attack on 14 July 2016 – when a lone nutcase drove a lorry into a crowd celebrating Bastille Day on the Promenade des Anglais – how could you beat that? The authorities then tried another policy: pooling the jihadists into UPRs, or radicalisation prevention units, whose name already leaves one wondering: what sense is there in trying to *prevent* the radicalisation of guys who've trained with the Islamic State's shock battalions in Syria? It's the dilemma of the prison system: how can you cut the jihadists off from the rest of the population, whom they risk contaminating, without creating new synergies in these smaller units, which are nothing other than the elite schools of terrorism? Micheron quotes the words of some returnees: 'As soon as there are more than three of us we name an emir.' 'Check it out: we jihadists are now on the inside, and what's going on in here is unprecedented in Europe. Historically, where have Islamist organisations regrouped? In prison, always! Prison is our bread and butter!' 'The key thing is how jihadism evolves in the next ten years. For me it's clear that the next al-Adnani will be European – French, even – and that he's now in a French prison.' (Killed in August 2016, al-Adnani was the spokesperson and ideologue of the Islamic State. It was he who, in response to the international coalition's first strikes on Syria and Iraq, gave the speech on 21 September 2014 that was quoted by Olivia Ronen at the hearing with former president Hollande: 'If you can kill a disbelieving American or European – especially the evil, dirty French – then trust Allah! Hit his head with a stone, slit his throat, run him over with your car, throw him from a high place, poison or strangle him!')

The book from the start?

Listening to Micheron, who speaks from the perspective of a historian, I think of an astonishing sentence uttered by Salah Abdeslam at the beginning of the trial and which, to my knowledge, went largely without comment: 'Everything you say about us jihadists is like reading the last page of a book. What you should do is read the book from the start.' I don't know where he got such a strong image, but until today it's one of the two answers I retain to the question that comes up again and again: What do you expect from this trial? The other was said by Pierre-Sylvain, a survivor of the Bataclan: 'I expect what happened to us to become a collective narrative.' Writing this collective narrative, reading the book from the start, are two immense ambitions. Beyond reach, no doubt. But that's why we're here.

The dry season

The conspiracy café

In police jargon, the thicket under the A86 motorway that served as the second-to-last hideout of the commando leader Abdelhamid Abaaoud is called the 'conspiracy bush' – the last being the squat in the Paris suburb of Saint-Denis where he was shot dead in a police raid on 18 November 2015. Terrorists' hideouts are referred to as 'conspiracy flats'. Used like this as an adjective, the word conspiracy has become a private joke among aficionados of the trial. Some of us call the bistro on Place Dauphine where we meet before the hearings the conspiracy café – 'See you tomorrow morning at the conspiracy café?' It's not just the journalists with a penchant for black humour who talk like that, but also plaintiffs, ex-Bataclan hostages – a small, informal group of people who come to the V13 proceedings every day and have in common the fact that they find them as addictive as a series. That said, for the past week you have to *really* be hooked to come every day. In late November we entered a dry season of the trial, in which investigators from the DGSE and the DGSI – the French foreign and homeland security agencies – and above all the Belgian police testify one after the other. Of course they have interesting things to say, but for their own safety they're heard under the cover of anonymity, that is to say by videoconference with their faces blurred. My colleagues on the press benches sigh.

The gendarmerie in Vesoul

Still, there was Bernard Bajolet. The former head of the DGSE, Bajolet is a nondescript man in his sixties. As a good spymaster he has no taste for the light, nevertheless he's come in person, with his face uncovered. When asked where he lives, he replies: 'Let's just say: the Vesoul police station.' Go figure. Everyone laughs, but the rest is less funny. What he says point-blank, without trying to shift the blame, is that his services completely screwed up. Let's backtrack. Since the beginning of 2014 it was known that Europe, and France in particular, faced the threat of massive, organised attacks. And several of the future terrorists – six or seven of the ten members of the V13 commando, Bajolet says coldly – were known as well. The most dangerous of them is Abdelhamid Abaaoud, whom we last saw at the wheel of a four-by-four, towing *kafir* corpses in the dust. That video makes him a hero for his Molenbeek friends, who play it over and over in the café Les Béguines, as if he'd won the Eurovision Song Contest. It also gets him a promotion. In early 2015 he joins the Amn al-Kharji, the Islamic

State's external operations wing dedicated to terrorist operations abroad. Just before Bajolet, two homeland security agents with the code names 948SI and 1310SI had come to detail the wing's organisation chart. Highly structured and hierarchical, the cell is headed by Osama Atar – the brother of Yassine Atar who's in the box – but it's Abaaoud who recruits and trains the candidates for the suicide operations being prepared in Europe. He's the operations manager. The French agencies – and not just the French – know this so well that in January 2015 they join forces with the Belgian Federal Police, the CIA and Mossad to catch him in Athens by sealing off an entire neighbourhood. Except that they don't catch him. After that Abaaoud disappears from the radar. The DGSE and DGSI agree that he's somewhere in Syria, and pin their hopes on him being killed in a bomb strike. No one suspects that from where he is in Raqqa he's mobilising his entire Molenbeek gang, or that starting in the summer he'll be coordinating the return of the members of the future commando from Syria to Belgium. No one sees any of this taking place. And no one really pays attention to the testimony of a petty jihadist named Reda Hame, who, picked up in August 2015 on his return from Syria, divulges what Abaaoud is planning in the hope of lightening his sentence: 'He's going to choose an easy target, a place where there are a lot of people. A concert hall. A rock concert. And,' he stresses, 'it's going to happen very soon.' In short, a complete cock-up on all fronts, Bajolet admits with dejected, rather striking honesty.

The Belgian investigators

The same cannot be said of the Belgian investigators. Much is expected from their depositions, as it was in Belgium that the attacks were prepared, eight of the accused are Belgian, and they were tracked down and arrested in Belgium. In short, even if the attacks took place on French soil, V13 is first and foremost a Belgian event. The Belgian investigators didn't do any better than their French counterparts, worse if anything, but unlike them they dodge questions, pass the buck – 'That wasn't my department, my colleagues can explain it much better than I can . . . ' – and what's more they lack the guts to be present at the trial. So we listen to their voices off-screen as they scroll through their PowerPoint presentations – occasionally jazzed up with animations showing a little plane flying from a Turkish flag to a Dutch flag to depict a journey from Istanbul to Amsterdam – from a meeting room in an administrative building in Brussels. It's a question of security, their superiors argue. Except that, as Abdeslam's lawyer Olivia Ronen points out, they didn't have the same qualms when it came to appearing on Belgian TV. The result: whether on their own decision or on their lawyers' advice, five defendants announce that if that's how things stand, they won't appear in court either. And so until further notice the sessions continue with the glass box half empty.

Five empty chairs

A court case where the defendants refuse to appear is quite a thing. It's their right, they can't be forced to show up, nevertheless in addition to stripping the hearings of some of their interest, it lengthens them considerably. You can't start without sending a bailiff to summon them to appear, and then you have to wait for him to come back empty-handed. This whole merry-go-round takes half an hour, which everyone has built into their schedules: the hearings now start with their own recess. I have to walk on eggshells here because of the presumption of innocence, still it can be said that the five defendants who, like Klaus Barbie in the past, have chosen the empty chair policy – Salah Abdeslam, Mohamed Abrini, Sofien Ayari, Osama Krayem and Mohamed Bakkali – are the biggest fish in this case. One can discuss how involved they were in the V13 attacks, but not whether or not they're terrorists. The upshot is that the only ones left in the box are the underlings, the ones who at least stand a chance of coming away with a milder sentence, and who for this reason are keeping their noses clean. And three of them aren't even in the box at all but in front of it: Abdellah Chouaa, Ali Oulkadi, Hamza Attou. These three intrigue me. I look at them, sitting in a row on their folding seats. They look like beaten dogs, students in detention. If one talks to another under his breath, the third bends over so as not to be left out.

Sometimes they laugh. They take notes. They come and go like us. We pass them in the hall, in the walkways. They hug the walls, keeping a low profile. One day the hearing started late because all the defendants have to be present before things can begin, and Hamza Attou was missing. Everyone waited for Hamza Attou. When he finally arrived, he explained sheepishly that his metro had been stuck between two stations, it really wasn't his fault. It's fine this time, the judge Périès said with his benevolent schoolmaster air, but in future, be sure to be here on time. After hearing him tell his story during the personality examinations, it's impossible to wish any harm on Hamza Attou. The same goes for Ali Oulkadi and Abdellah Chouaa. These three may not be saints, but it's only by chance that they're here at all, and I wonder how they cope with the terrible hard luck of finding themselves alongside dangerous terrorists in this gigantic trial that is being watched all over the world. What their lives must be like during these nine months. Where they live, what they hope for and what they fear, what they tell their families. I wonder all of that, and if I could get my courage up I'd ask them.

Three folding seats

Far from Molenbeek

It's always dark when Abdellah Chouaa leaves the Palais de Justice. Ever since he got to Paris he's wanted to see the Champs-Élysées, but it's a long way away and he doesn't dare to make the trip, he's afraid he'll get lost or be recognised, so for the time being he sticks to this one route: metro 14 from Châtelet station to Saint-Ouen, from there metro 13 to Basilique Saint-Denis, where he takes bus number 153 to get home. Home is a garden shed behind the house of an elderly woman whose living room he has to cross to reach the backyard. A hundred square feet, 600 euros per month. On his own, with no contacts, no payslips and problems that are difficult to acknowledge, he'd never have been able to find anything like it without the help of his lawyer, and at least in that respect he's been lucky. But he's got a second rent to pay in Belgium, 700 euros, petrol costs to get from Paris to Brussels and back every weekend, food – even if he shops in Brussels where it's cheaper – and all the other costs of a family of five. His mother and sisters help out a bit, each pitching in 50 euros a month, but things can't go on like this indefinitely. Before it all started he had a real job, delivering ice blocks to the airport where they were put in the luggage holds, but now he spends every Sunday at the markets selling clothes that have fallen off the back of a lorry. Under the counter, he confesses to the court, which doesn't have the heart to reproach him for it. The day of our discussion he's just sold his car for 3,700 euros, which will have to last him until the end of the trial in May. Assuming, of course, that at the end of the trial he's not sent back to prison: that would be so terrible he would rather not have to think about it.

'Some of Daddy's friends did some really stupid things'

Like Hamza Attou and Ali Oulkadi, Abdellah Chouaa appears at V13 subject to judicial supervision, accused but not detained, and obliged to be present at every session. Day after day, these three men from Molenbeek, all in their thirties, who are no strangers to petty crime and above all to bad luck, sit in front of the glass box where the eleven 'real' defendants appear. He, Abdellah Chouaa, never turns round to look at them or speak to them. He doesn't want anything to do with them – especially not with his former friend Mohamed Abrini, one of the big shots in this case and whose fault it is that he's here in the first place. Abdellah Chouaa was unfortunate enough to have driven Abrini to Brussels-Zaventem Airport on 23 June 2015, and then to have picked him up in Paris on 16 July. Between those two dates he received frequent phone calls from Abrini from exotic numbers in Laos, Bhutan, Guinea and Russia – all actually emanating from telephone shops in Syria. During the investigation he swore he thought Abrini was going on holiday in Turkey and had no idea that he was in fact leaving for Syria. Instead of minimising Abdellah Chouaa's role, however – as he could easily have done – Abrini never stopped driving the nail in deeper: how could Chouaa not have known where he was going and why? he said: his radicalisation was an open secret in Molenbeek. I don't want to weigh in here, nevertheless for Chouaa and the two others to have been released after just a few months in detention, the evidence against them must be slim indeed. Weighty enough, however, to oblige them to appear at V13 and turn their lives into a nightmare. Abdellah Chouaa tells his eldest son, aged ten, that he only comes home at weekends because he's found a job in Paris, in security, but he's always afraid that one of his boy's friends at school will see his photo in the newspaper or on TV and say in front of everyone: 'So your father's a terrorist?' Maybe he should do the same as Ali Oulkadi, who summoned the courage to explain to his eldest daughter, also ten, that some men did some really stupid things, that Daddy knew one of these men and is in big trouble because of it.

A plate of pasta in a garden shed

Ali Oulkadi is the man of the last link in the chain, the one who drove Salah Abdeslam – whom Hamza Attou and Mohammed Amri had brought back from Paris during the night – from one place to another in Brussels on the morning of 14 November. No one really suspects these three of being terrorists, nevertheless there's no getting around the fact that they were friends with a terrorist and helped him escape. Hamza Attou and Ali Oulkadi were regulars at the notorious café Les Béguines in Molenbeek, run by Abdeslam's brother Brahim. There they spent most of their time smoking cannabis – and selling it. But even if, like the other two, Abdellah Chouaa has a modest criminal record, he's keen to draw a discreet line between himself and his two companions in misfortune. Whereas the other defendants all cultivate the same trainers-tracksuit-hoodie look, he wears a light-coloured suit that's a little too lightweight for the time of year and a thin white polo-neck jumper under his white shirt: if anything he looks like an estate agent or telephone salesman, but not some piece of riffraff. Every day the three of them meet at 11.30 a.m. in front of the Palais de Justice, where they enter under police escort and to curious looks that send shivers down their spine. Ali Oulkadi doesn't have Abdellah Chouaa's luck, and hasn't found a place he can sleep. He moves from one cheap hotel to another depending on their promotional offers, and sometimes, when he's got nowhere else to go, Abdellah Chouaa puts him up in his shed. They cook some pasta, Abdellah Chouaa gives himself a shot of insulin because he's diabetic, then they lie in bed and tell each other about the lives they dream of when all of this is over: a house, a garden, a more or less steady job, seeing their children grow up. Smoking a joint or two, but only at the weekend.

Nino and Marius

The other day Ali Oulkadi and I met and talked during a recess in the proceedings, sitting on a bench in a walkway of the courthouse. He told me how terrible the five weeks of the plaintiffs' testimony had been for them. Almost every day a bereaved father or mother would fire a remark at the defendants' box, lumping them all together as if they, Abdellah Chouaa, Hamza Attou and Ali Oulkadi, had gunned down their children with Kalashnikovs. They'd each had to fight the urge to stand up and shout: 'I'm not with them! I didn't do anything!' At that moment a woman came up to us to tell me that she'd been reading and enjoying my columns. She was one of the plaintiffs, and wanted to know if I remembered her testimony. Unfortunately I didn't, she'd probably given it on one of the rare days I hadn't been present. Hoping to refresh my memory, she said: 'I came to the stand with my two grandsons.' 'Nino and Marius,'

Ali Oulkadi interjected. I don't know if the woman recognised him or not, but she smiled at him and nodded: 'Yes: Nino and Marius.' As she walked away, a glimmer of pure joy flashed across Ali Oulkadi's face, because someone had spoken to him like he was a normal person. 'Nino and Marius,' he repeated softly, as if the names of these little boys whose father had been murdered at the Bataclan were those of his own children, and because he'd been granted, fleetingly, perhaps by mistake but that was already something, the right to grieve like everyone else.

Which is worse?

In custody

At 9.57 p.m., as pieces of Samy Amimour, pulverised by his suicide vest, rained down like confetti on the pit at the Bataclan, Azdyne Amimour, his father, was watching the France–Germany football match, which was continuing at the Stade de France as if nothing had happened, on TF1. To avoid triggering a panic the channel had not interrupted the broadcast, with the result that those watching the match on TV were among the last to learn about the massacres that had begun half an hour earlier at the gates of the stadium. Azdyne remembers a loud bang at the start of the second half, the strange hesitation of left-back Patrice Evra on the pitch, and then nothing special. It was only at the end of the match, which the French team won 2–0, that he learned what had taken place. He called his wife to make sure nothing had happened to their youngest daughter, who was out with some friends that night. He didn't think for a minute that Samy might have been involved in the attacks, he says, for the paradoxical reason that he'd gone to Syria to take part in the jihad. Since he was in Syria, he couldn't be in Paris. So Azdyne wasn't overly worried until the night of 15 November, when a dozen men in ninja garb burst through their door, handcuffed him, his wife and his daughter, and hustled them off to the DGSI head-quarters. There he was interrogated for four days, without having the first idea – he says – why. It was only at the end of his custody that the public prosecutor told him, firstly, that his son had been killed at the Bataclan, and secondly, that he himself had killed several dozen people, in cold blood and with a certain pleasure.

Truth and lies

The books *Strangers in Their Own Land: Young Jews in Germany and Austria Today* and *Born Guilty: Children of Nazi Families* * gather interviews with the children of Jewish World War II deportees on the one hand, and the children of Nazi parents on the other. The questions underlying the two works: Is the burden that weighs on these groups equal? Is their suffering equally worthy of compassion? Answering yes may require some effort, but it's an effort that morality and reason demand: sons are not responsible for the crimes of their fathers. Regarding the inverse case, however, things are more complicated: when a child becomes a murderer, the family is invariably

* Peter Sichrovsky: *Strangers in Their Own Land: Young Jews in Germany and Austria Today*, Basic Books, 1986; *Born Guilty: Children of Nazi Families*, Basic Books, 1988.

thought to have something to do with it. That's why when Azdyne Amimour appeared at the trial to shed light on his son's life, he was asked not only for an explanation of his son's behaviour, but also for an account of his own. He's seventy-four, exhausted, evasive, dressed in an old army jacket, but also, in his own words, 'cool and relaxed'. This comment did not go down particularly well with the court, and neither did his bearing when, after accepting the chair he was offered, he leaned back on it as if he were at his local watering hole. Between France and Algeria he's done practically every job in the book, worked in the cinema and the garment industry, run his own shops, with his share of nice cars and bankruptcies. In any case he's neither poor nor overly devout. He rarely goes to the mosque, and has never taken his children there. He would even get dressed up as Father Christmas when Christmas time rolled around. As a child Samy was gentle and affectionate, if somewhat downhearted, then as a teenager he was introverted, Azdyne says. He could sense that his son was unhappy, but was unsure how to help him. He hoped it would pass, and most of the time it did. But then it didn't. What followed was the horribly stereotypical process of radicalisation that so many parents, Muslim or not, describe with the same sense of helplessness. Samy not only starts praying, he explains to his father that if his business is going downhill it's because he himself doesn't pray, and because he lives the life of a non-believer. Samy starts wearing the qamis, and piles up pamphlets in his room with titles like 'Yes! I've Converted to Islam', 'How to Strengthen My Faith' and 'The Signs of the End Times'. And he repeats over and over that 9/11 was a Jewish plot. His father isn't at all happy about this – even if he tends to go along with his son on the last point – but he prefers not to get the boy's back up. He prefers to think that it's better for him to stay in his room and watch Salafist preachers on the internet than go out and drink or do drugs. When Samy leaves for Syria in the autumn of 2013, Azdyne does his best to believe he's going there to do 'humanitarian work', and he astonishes everyone at the trial when he calls the al-Nusra Front – the Syrian branch of al-Qaeda that his son had gone to join – an 'association'. Still, it's increasingly difficult to hide the fact that there's something dodgy going on. The Kalashnikovs lined up behind the young man belong to friends, he explains when his parents call him on Skype, but that doesn't reassure them. Strange friends, they think. Two years later they'll learn that those same friends were the group of torturers led by Abdelhamid Abaaoud from which the 13 November commando was recruited. In June 2014 Azdyne has an insight, and takes the courageous if slightly crazy decision to leave for Syria himself and bring back his son. This trip, which in any case came to nothing, is somewhat shrouded in mystery. On his return Azdyne gave an interview to *Le Monde* in which he includes all of the obligatory elements found in the accounts of parents visiting their jihadist children: the wait at the Turkish-Syrian border, haggling with the smugglers, switching vehicles, meeting the emir of his son's brigade . . . Later, two days after the attacks, Azdyne came up with a new account, confessing to the DGSI investigators that, although it's true he went to Turkey, he never set foot in Syria. Still later he returned to his first version: Yes I went there. That's the version he sticks to in the trial, at the cost of many inconsistencies and in an increasingly aggressive cross-examination. Finally chief prosecutor Camille Hennetier – impeccable as always – reminds the court that Azdyne is a witness, not a defendant, adding that yes, his lie to the DGSI was child-ish, but it was also human and forgivable. Who in the same situation would brag that he'd gone to Syria? I agree with her, and believe the key element of Azdyne's story: his sad encounter with Samy in the rocky Syrian badlands, the boy walking on crutches, his icy stare, definitively gone over to the other side. Then his return, sick at heart, to Turkey and France. He'd never see his son again. At the morgue his body would no longer have the shape of a body. And the last images that exist of the sad little boy to whom he gave presents dressed as Father Christmas are contained in the Islamic State's video claiming responsibility for the attacks, showing him laughing while decapitating a prisoner.

Two fathers, again

I've already spoken about Georges Salines, whose daughter Lola was killed at the Bataclan, and with whom

I've gradually become friends as the trial progresses. Two years after the attacks he received a letter from Azdyne Amimour saying: 'I'd like to talk to you about this tragic event, because I too feel like a victim because of my son.' Salines was initially taken aback, but he accepted. What came out of their discussions is a book in two voices, *Il nous reste les mots* (All we have left is words). Two bereaved fathers talk to each other. As there were three killers, there's a one in three chance that one man's son fired the bullet that killed the other man's daughter. Reading their discussions, one wonders: which is worse? Having a son who murders or a daughter who's murdered? I get the impression that it's mainly Salines who asks this knotty question. Other, equally dizzying questions follow: would he be any better off in Azdyne's shoes? Would he have been able to stop his child on the path to disaster? By saying what, by doing what? And what about myself? If it were my daughter or son . . . ? I don't know, nobody knows. I only know that at midnight on 20 November 2015, Azdyne Amimour and his wife left police custody, took a taxi home, remained silent for the whole journey, and never spoke to each other about their son again.

At the café Les Béguines

To drop the T

This is the objective of the lawyers whose clients are charged with criminal terrorist association: to drop the T for 'terrorist' and reduce their charge to criminal association tout court – for which the punishment is far less severe. In these last few days of the year before the trial breaks for two weeks, there's been a lot of talk about the notorious café Les Béguines, run by Brahim Abdeslam in Molenbeek. Who hung out there? Pretty much the whole gang, whether as waiters, dealers or regulars – many of them all three. What did they do there? Watch Islamic State videos? Yes. Brahim played them in a loop on his computer, closing the lid whenever someone he didn't know came in. But what about the others? Did they watch them too? Were there 'viewing sessions' of these atrocious images: the beheading of the American journalist James Foley; the Jordanian pilot burnt alive in a cage; and their favourite video since they knew the star: Abdelhamid Abaaoud, their childhood friend, their brother, at the wheel of his pickup, towing corpses in the Syrian dust and laughing with his psychopathic little gremlin's face, inviting viewers to come and have some fun? And what about

Mohammed Amri, Hamza Attou and Ali Oulkadi, who dealt and smoked at Les Béguines and occasionally helped out behind the bar? Did they sit in a circle around the computer and engage in spiritual communion while watching the images – as the expression 'viewing session' suggests, and as the prosecution is trying to establish? Or did they just go about their work, casting an indifferent look at the screen from time to time, the way people who don't really care about football take in a match, as the defence lawyers argue? Were they criminals by proximity, the way others are victims by ricochet? Another question, with serious implications for everyone concerned: did they go down into the cellar? That's where Brahim shut himself away for his long Skype talks with Abaaoud, who was starting to organise the attacks from Raqqa. Because those who can be proven to have joined him in the cellar are done for: their T is there to stay.

'We asked him'

After the attacks, the Belgian investigators searched the café Les Béguines with a very precise objective in mind. In one of the 'conspiracy flats' used by Salah Abdeslam during his escape, a fork was found bearing DNA traces belonging to Ali Oulkadi, who helped him on the last leg of his escape. At first sight this is a damning detail, but Ali Oulkadi's lawyers argue that the fork most certainly came from the café Les Béguines, where everyone handled the cutlery. So the mission of the investigators – who for one reason or another belonged not to the anti-terrorist police force but to the financial services – consisted of going to the café, seizing and putting seals on thirty-one forks, the analysis of which revealed nothing conclusive, and then going back home. According to their report, searching this café, from which all the logistics of the V13 attacks were organised over several months, took a total of fifteen minutes. PFB 446 906 682, the Belgian policeman who came to present its findings – or rather, who did not come to present its findings, as he was testifying from Brussels via video link with his face blurred – had his back to the wall, in particular when he was asked why his team hadn't had the curiosity to check the cellar. 'What? There was a cellar?' The next day it was the turn of his colleague PFB 440 232 779. In February 2015 his team had taken Brahim Abdeslam, who was in possession of a booklet entitled 'Parental Permission to Take Part in the Jihad' and suspected of planning a terrorist attack, into custody. And then they released him. 'Why?' 'Because,' the officer replied, 'there was nothing in his interrogation to suggest that he had any terrorist intentions.' 'But,' interjected the presiding judge in surprise, 'on what basis did you conclude that?' 'Well, *we asked him*.'

'The Clains? Good copy.'

It's known, then, that they watched execution videos at Les Béguines. And that they listened to nasheeds – those

VI3

jihadist chants to music that's more or less like rap. As for the lyrics, here's a sample:

We have to hit France,
It needs humiliation
We must inflict suffering
And death by the thousands.

This nasheed was composed, performed and broadcast from Raqqa by two brothers, Fabien and Jean-Michel Clain, in celebration of the *Charlie Hebdo* massacre in January 2015. Emblematic figures of French jihadism and in charge of the Islamic State's propaganda, they most likely died in 2019, after the caliphate was routed. But as no one can say that for certain they're among the defendants *in absentia* at this trial – those who failed to respond to the court summons 'without a valid excuse' as Judge Périès said at the start. Big fish, in any case, about whom a journalist I admire, but who made me swear not to name her if I quoted her, effused: 'The Clains? Good copy.' The court allotted two long days to their story, which began in 1999. Originally they were Catholics from Normandy. Their mother taught the catechism, the boys propped up the walls, rapped and dealt drugs on their housing estate in Alençon. Their sister Marie-Diana, who testifies from her prison cell, describes all of the children as driven by a strong desire for spirituality. They look for a meaning to life, but can't find it in the Bible. The parish priest in Alençon has nothing to offer.

Someone talks to them about the Quran and, miraculously, in two weeks they've all converted, with their mother the catechist leading the way. Hard-core Islam: the walls of the flat are covered with photos of Mecca, curtains hang from the ceiling to divide the rooms in two, with one part for the men and one for the women. The women wear the burqa, which is still uncommon at the time. In the streets of Toulouse, where they've moved, this earns the family the nickname 'the Belphegor gang'. Like the Belgian city of Charleroi, Toulouse is a cradle of European Salafism. It was there that the jihadist Mohamed Merah murdered first three soldiers and then a teacher and three children in a Jewish school in 2012. The Clain family has close ties with the Merahs, and reveres Mohamed, this hero of Islamism, in a form of veneration widely shared in all French prisons. The two brothers are good talkers, sincere and charismatic – Fabien in particular. In a quarter of an hour, this big, warm, good-humoured young man can convince his listeners that Allah loves them and that he's the answer to all the questions they ask themselves and all the woes that beset them. Then the civil war in Syria starts. Jean-Michel is the first to go, then Fabien, then the whole clan: the mother, the sister and the sister's daughter Jennifer, who also testifies from her prison cell. Hers is a chilling testimony of a life devoted to radical Islam without ever having had a choice. Jennifer left school at fourteen, when she was fifteen her mother and uncles married her to a Salafist from Bayonne who was no older than she was. She gave birth to five children, one after the other. 'We didn't go to Syria because of the war,' she says, 'we went there to build a country, to bring up our children, to live our religion in a land of Islam and not a land of disbelief. For me the Islamic State wasn't a terrorist organisation.' To underscore this idealistic vision she describes Raqqa under the black flag: women and children confined to their houses, slaves sold at the market, executions on public squares displayed on giant screens in the middle of the street. 'And did the people approve of this?' 'Yes. Everyone did, everyone who was there. And if they didn't they'd never say it, it was too dangerous.' 'Then what made you leave? The ill treatment? The Jordanian pilot? The men with tied hands being slowly beheaded with knives?' 'No, frankly I had no problem with all of that. I thought it was normal.' 'What were your uncles doing there?' 'They were making music. Jean-Michel sang, and I think Fabien was a sound engineer . . .'

'Running towards your prey like a roaring lion'

Another nasheed by the Clains claims responsibility for the 13 November attacks:

> *Advance, advance. Advance, advance.*
> *Never retreat, never surrender*
> *Advance, advance, unconquered warrior, kill them sword in hand*

Kill the soldiers of the devil without wavering
Make them bleed right in their homes
Fear nothing, go straight to happiness
The field of battle and the field of honour
No more polemics or philosophy
Either you kill them or they'll kill you, you only stand to gain
Whoever opposes the sharia is lost
Even if he claims to be virtuous
So sever the heads of ignorance
Sever the heads of the vagrant soldiers
In this war you have everything to gain
One fine day your sweat and blood will bear witness
Fight until you meet the almighty
Running towards your prey like a roaring lion.

Under the Rojava sun

'On holiday in the Islamic State?'

Apart from the times when an entire family goes over to the other side, as was the case with the Clains, stories of radicalisation are generally told from the point of view of the dismayed parents, and they tend to be very similar. So I'll skim briefly over the first chapter of the account told to me by Anne and Pierre Martinez, a couple in their sixties, both of them educators, agnostic, open-minded, and as unprepared as could be for the moment when their son Antoine, at eighteen, starts taking the bits of chorizo sausage from his paella with a disgusted look on his face (Pierre's a pied noir of Spanish origin). Then he grows a big beard, starts wearing the qamis, and introduces his parents to Safia, the extremely young veiled girl whom he has just married religiously and who has not yet passed her baccalaureate exams when she gives birth to their first child. Anne and Pierre wonder what kind of a relationship they can have with a child raised with values so different from their own, but contrary to expectations things aren't bad at all. Antoine and Safia often entrust them with little Nadim, who adores them and whom they adore. They're not allowed to drink wine in front of him, but they can decorate the Christmas tree. They discover the reassuring notion of 'quietist Salafism', and repeat to themselves that their son is a quietist Salafist. Of course it would be better if he weren't, still it's not the end of the world, and no alarm signals go off when the little family of quietist Salafists, now larger with a second child, goes on holiday to Italy in the summer of 2015. Then the second chapter begins, much darker than the first. At first Antoine and Safia don't say where they are, then say they're not in Italy but in Syria, under the black flag of the Islamic State. Then Antoine explains to them that it's great to live under the black flag of the Islamic State, that they live in a nice flat in Mosul, in the Iraqi part of the caliphate, and that of course there are problems, violence and all that, but in a few months things will have stabilised and Papa and Maman will be able to come on holiday. 'On holiday?' Pierre chokes. 'In the Islamic State?' From that summer on, the Martinezes lead a double life. Continually hovering around the telephone, unable to sleep, only opening up to those who share their misfortune, they enter the cruel world of the parents of jihadists, who meet and swap stories about the stages of their children's radicalisation, rare bits of news they receive, and contacts at the DGSI. From one phone call to the next, Antoine's enthusiasm for the caliphate and the prospect of a family get-together in Mosul wanes. While he undergoes military training, Safia and their two little ones wait for him in a *madafa*, or house reserved for women – 'reserved' meaning they're confined there. Sometimes separated and sometimes reunited without ever knowing why, they soon no longer even try to hide the fact that they're scared to death, and much more of the Islamic State than of the government troops. Everyone's afraid in Mosul. When their third child is born, Antoine sobs to his parents: 'I don't want our children to grow up here, we want to come home, we want to surrender.' He finds a smuggler, but the smuggler takes their money and leaves the five of them at the side of the road before they reach the Turkish border. Antoine is arrested. It's 2018, total chaos, the fall of the caliphate, a time so dangerous that the Martinezes are relieved to learn that Safia and the children are now in a Kurdish-run prison camp in the desert region of Rojava, in north-eastern Syria.

In the camp

A prison camp, they think at first, must be relatively accessible and organised, a place the Red Cross and consular authorities have access to: the children will be repatriated, the parents will no doubt go to prison, but it's doable. The Martinezes approach the French Foreign Ministry again and again, but they're told that France no longer has diplomatic relations with Syria and there's nothing to be done. Nothing. Safia no longer has a phone, they're forbidden in the camp, but sometimes someone lends her one, and Anne and Pierre are not at all reassured to learn that on the day of his eighth birthday Nadim was beaten, stoned, and thrown on a rubbish heap by a gang of wild, haggard children. He's terrorised and no longer leaves their tent. Safia, who's insulted and threatened by women who've remained loyal to the Islamic State, is terrified as well. The Martinezes send all the money they can, they have to go through several less and less legal intermediaries, with the double risk of being swindled and prosecuted for financing terrorism. But it's the only way to ensure that the children have mineral water – and not the dirty water that gives the internees dysentery in this camp where everyone literally walks in shit – food supplements and nappies, because Safia has just given birth to a fourth child. They spend their days in their tent, on the ground, leaving it as little as possible because it's dangerous outside: robberies, assaults and rape are common. The kerosene stoves risk catching fire so they're turned off at night, although it's minus ten degrees in the winter but plus forty in the summer. In May 2019, after a trial that lasts half an hour, Antoine is sentenced to death by a court in Baghdad. The last anyone heard he was in a prison where sixty or seventy men are crammed into cells measuring no more than six hundred square feet. The Martinezes then summon their courage and make contact with an Austrian NGO active in Syria, and at the end of an obstacle course made up of a long series of offices, small glasses of very sweet tea and numerous bribes, they obtain the stamped permit that gets them as far as al-Roj refugee camp, with their suitcases full of gifts and schoolbooks. The Austrians are allowed in but they aren't, not even their suitcases. The Kurdish guards are nice enough, and tell them with an apologetic look that no, French people simply can't enter: orders from above. They come back the next day and exchange a few words and kisses through the fence with Nadim and two of his brothers. They never thought they'd ever experience anything so heartbreaking. This lasts for five minutes, then the guards come with their machine guns and take away the children who are in tears. Before he leaves, Pierre walks along the fence around the camp: less than fifteen minutes. His grandchildren's entire lives take place within this perimeter. The littlest, who was born in the camp, has never known anything else.

A jihadist dumping ground

The Martinezes return home disheartened and distraught, but with a certain measure of hope because much is being done in France at the highest state level to repatriate the mothers and children. The mothers will be tried by French courts, the children entrusted to foster homes. And then an opinion poll reveals that a majority of French people are worried about these returnees. The process is immediately frozen. Foreign Minister Jean-Yves Le Drian goes to Baghdad in the hopes of passing the buck to Iraq, and is told that the country is not a 'jihadist dumping ground'. Since 2019 repatriations have been taking place 'on a case-by-case basis', as the official word has it, that is to say arbitrarily, in dribs and drabs, separating the mothers and their children – something no other country does. Even now there are still around two hundred French children in al-Roj, children who did not choose to have jihadist parents and who are growing up in an environment of abject poverty, violence and, as often as not, blind veneration of a father whom they consider a martyr. They're extremely unhappy and of course potentially dangerous – leading some people to think that it's better to let them croak where they are. One could think the opposite: that repatriating them is not only a humanitarian duty but also a security precaution. That's what their grandparents think, and with them dozens of magistrates, politicians, child psychiatrists like Serge Hefez, whom I know and respect, and lawyers like Marie Dosé, who works with Judith Lévy on Ali Oulkadi's defence. A committed professional, Marie Dosé has put no end of energy into this battle. It was through her, in her office, that I met the Martinezes. She and her colleagues multiply their appeals, petitions and warnings, all in vain. The officials they seek out look the other way, telling them that things are more complicated than they seem. Of course they're complicated, no one doubts that, but between taking charge of these children, with all of the difficulties that entails, and abandoning them under the deadly Rojava sun with no other fate than to become human bombs, sick with hatred for the country that let them down, I think, like Anne, Pierre, Marie, Serge and the others, that the first option is better than the second, and even though I'm not big on signing petitions, this one I'm going to sign.

Taqîya

Remaining silent

The defendants face another round of questioning. At the start of the hearing, Osama Krayem's lawyer asks to read a letter in which his client says: 'No one here is trying to understand, and I do not believe that giving my opinion about what I am accused of will change anything in the court's decision. I have thus taken the decision to remain silent until the end of the proceedings.' In what follows, Osama Krayem's cross-examination consists of a series of questions from, in the usual order, the presiding judge and his assistants, the public prosecutors, the lawyers for the plaintiffs, and then the defence. These are long and detailed sessions, at the end of which the court turns to the accused for form's sake and just in case he's changed his mind. But he hasn't, and remains impassive and mute, staring into space without blinking. One may wonder which of these two strategies for rejecting the court's authority – refusing to appear or appearing and refusing to speak – is more effective. In my opinion it's the second: there's something deeply destabilising about a silent physical presence. Everything takes place in front of a wall. Fine-featured, with long,

straight, black hair parted in the middle and a full beard
under his mask, Osama Krayem is a thirty-year-old
Swedish native, raised in Malmö in a Syrian, Lebanese or
Palestinian family – it's not entirely clear which, but with
him nothing is clear – who, after assiduously dedicating
his teens to football, started to practise his religion every
bit as assiduously. He does not, however, accept the
word 'radicalisation': 'In religion,' he said, back when he
was still speaking, 'you either take it all or leave it all. If
the Quran says something is right, then it's right, even
if the rest of humanity says the opposite.' In August 2014
Krayem answers the call of Abu Mohammad al-Adnani,
who has just proclaimed the caliphate, and leaves for
Syria to 'do humanitarian work', as attested by his presence among the fifteen bearded men in combat fatigues
in attendance when the Jordanian fighter pilot is burnt
alive in a cage – the most atrocious of the atrocious
Islamic State videos. In the spring of 2015 he's noticed
by Osama Atar, the caliphate's head of external operations. According to a letter to his sister, Krayem has
learned 'some amazing stuff' from Atar, and now seeks
'to do the best deed, the one that makes Allah the happiest'. 'The best deed, the one that makes Allah the
happiest' is a suicide operation conceived by the top
leaders at the external operations wing and organised by
Abdelhamid Abaaoud from Raqqa, on which he sets out
from Syria in mid-September 2015. He enters Europe
via Greece on a false Syrian passport in the company of
two other Syrian-trained fighters, Sofien Ayari and

Ahmad Alkhald. The three regroup in Vienna, where Salah Abdeslam picks them up on 3 October to take them to Belgium – though in writing this I'm getting ahead of myself: we're not there yet. In fact, Krayem was only indirectly involved in the Paris attacks, as he was saving himself for the Brussels metro bombing on 22 March 2016. But like Salah Abdeslam in the Paris attack, he changed his mind at the last minute and didn't activate the bomb he was carrying in his backpack, although it's unlikely he'll tell us why.

A decent man

As his brother and sister failed to respond to the summons, Osama Krayem's defence lawyer found only one witness he could cite in his favour: a retired Belgian teacher and volunteer prison worker who'd given Krayem French lessons for four years while he was in custody. 175 lessons, each lasting one and a half hours – so 260 hours one-on-one, he calculates – which gives him a certain authority in talking about his student. Dressed in a grey parka, he's a little grey himself, and exudes an air of peace and precision. They began by studying a book in Hergé's Tintin comic series, *Tintin and the Broken Ear*, he says, and continued with Antoine de Saint-Exupéry's *The Little Prince*. Krayem struck him as a thoughtful, even-tempered young man, keen to be seen as reliable and honest, someone who kept his word. He was a willing pupil, and a bond of respect and trust developed between the two over the course of the lessons. 'Leaving aside the horrible things he's done, Mr Krayem is a very humane person.' The sentence met with a storm of condemnation. Isn't extolling the humanity of someone who was part of the Islamic State's cruellest brigade similar to praising an Auschwitz commander who *in other respects* is a loving father and caring husband? 'Perhaps,' says the teacher with unshakeable gentleness. 'I don't want to play down the seriousness of his actions, I'm simply talking about the man I got to know over four years. Maybe he's not the best of men, but he's decent and humane. If we want to live in a democracy, there must be people who speak up for the accused.' There must be, yes. But then another lawyer reads this passage from a letter Krayem sent to his brother: 'The *kuffar* are our enemies. Hate them with all of your heart, but don't show it.' What if the decency and humanity noted by this teacher, for all his moral rectitude and grey Gore-tex, were *taqîya*, pure and simple?

Body Snatchers

We who follow this trial now use the word as if we'd known it all our lives. Some lawyers use it too much. Instead of saying 'a lie', they say *taqîya*, it's classier. However, *taqîya* isn't quite the same thing as when a defendant lies to a judge. Historically it refers to the way believers concealed their religious practices when they were not free to live them openly. What the Shiites did under the Abbasid caliphs in the eighth century, what the Muslims and Marrano Jews did in Catholic Spain in the fifteenth. For today's jihadists, who live and work like submarines in a society they hate and wish to destroy, such concealment has become second nature. To fool the unbelievers, you have to blend in with them. You have to pass yourself off as a nice Muslim who's happy to pray without bothering anyone, in full respect of the social pact. *Taqîya* is a powerful vehicle of paranoia, one that haunts the nights of judges and anti-terrorist policemen: is a harmless or sincerely repentant look in fact proof that the person giving it is hugely dangerous? It's like in the 1950s sci-fi film *Invasion of the Body Snatchers*, when the inhabitants of a peaceful town are possessed by evil aliens one by one. Nothing distinguishes the real Earthlings – if there still are any – from the beings who've replaced them. A cold monster could well be hiding behind your neighbour's familiar face. In its rigorous version, Islam forbids drinking alcohol, smoking, gambling, chasing women and listening to music. What, then, would a jihadist do to dissimulate the fact that he's about to commit a monstrous crime? Drink alcohol, smoke, gamble, chase women, listen to music – like the suicide bombers of 9/11 or, for that matter, like Salah Abdeslam.

The boys on Leros

At the end of August 2016, I spent some time on the small Greek island of Leros. Much to the displeasure of its inhabitants, it had been turned into a hotspot where migrants – mainly Syrians fleeing Bashar al-Assad's regime – were received and sorted. I ran a writing workshop, where I got to know five of these very young men, and collected their stories of their odyssey as best I could. Their trek involved long, exhausting walks, hunger and thirst, greedy and sometimes treacherous smugglers, crossing from Izmir to Leros in a partly deflated, overloaded Zodiac with the ever-present threat of drowning. These boys impressed me with their courage and maturity. In my book *Yoga* I wrote a longer portrait of one. And of course as we reconstructed, step by step, the journey taken by Osama Krayem, Sofien Ayari and Ahmad Alkhald to Europe, I thought of that boy and his trip. Going by the names Ahmed, Naïm and Mounir, Krayem and his two comrades also arrived on Leros in a Zodiac, exactly one year before I did, spending a few days there before being registered and continuing to Vienna, where they were picked up by Salah Abdeslam. When I think about it, nothing distinguished them from the boys I met there. They were no doubt just as endearing, their stories just as convincing. They too had arrived from Syria claiming to have been driven out by Bashar, whereas in fact they were following orders from the

Islamic State to bring fire and terror to the heart of Europe. Would I have been wary of them if they'd participated in my workshop? Or would I have dedicated pages full of confidence and compassion to Osama Krayem?

The epidemic of silence

Bakkali is silent

Things may change, in fact they're certain to change, but for now the trial is in a rut. Since the Christmas holidays two of the accused have fallen ill with Covid, resulting in a two-week break that wreaks havoc on the hallowed schedule. Above all, the box is ravaged by a worrying epidemic of silence. After Osama Krayem, it's now Mohamed Bakkali's turn. During the personality examinations in the autumn, Bakkali made a strong impression with his solid presence, his deep, steady voice and the thoughtful ease with which he spoke. As he too travelled to Syria he's accused of helping out with logistics, that is renting hideouts and driving the killers around, both for the Paris attacks and for the planned attack on the Belgian Thalys high-speed train in August 2015. The Thalys shooting was foiled, but Bakkali was nevertheless tried and, although he never stopped declaring his innocence, given a 25-year prison sentence which he has appealed. As his appeal is suspensive, until further notice he's the only one of the defendants with a clean record; however, his obvious intelligence will always be an aggravating circumstance: if a guy of his calibre is implicated, one can't help thinking, it's not for shuttling people back and forth like Mohammed Amri or Hamza Attou. So a lot is expected of his deposition. But even before the first question he stands up and explains why he won't be answering: 'I've already been tried and judged. I played the game and it didn't change a thing. I was convicted without a scrap of evidence for something I didn't do. I know that no matter what I say my word is worthless here, and I don't have the strength to fight or explain myself any more. For that reason I will exercise my right to silence.' A long pause. The presiding judge processes the information. Like us, he feels the trial is going to pieces. Sensing that after Krayem the dominoes are likely to fall one after the other and that it will be increasingly difficult to say the show must go on nonetheless, he tries to get the rebel to come round. 'That is your inalienable right (this is true). But you know that such a decision could work against you.' 'Everything works against me. No matter what I do.' 'But you did appeal. You know there are such things as acquittals on appeal . . .' The attempt is pitiful, Bakkali has no need for irony: 'In such a serious terrorism case?' Sigh. Since things must keep moving the interrogation proceeds, and each party in turn poses questions from which no one hopes for an answer.

Ayari speaks

Nothing was expected of Sofien Ayari. Everyone present was resigned to the fact that, like Osama Krayem and Mohamed Bakkali, he'd button up. It is no coincidence that these three are the biggest fish in the box, seasoned fighters of the Islamic State. If they say nothing, it's because they'd have a lot to say. So it was with the peeved attitude of someone who's preparing to question a wall that the presiding judge launched into Ayari's questioning. Surprise: the accused stands up and says that today, exceptionally, he will speak. Why? Because, he says, he owes it to 'the woman who lost her daughter on one of the terraces, and who reminded me of my mother. She said that we could have been her children, little angels that she'd have held by the hand on their way to school. She asked, "What could have happened for these children to turn out like that?" I can't bring her daughter back. I can't make her happy. But I can try to give her an answer. I owe her that.' So he talked. For six hours. Although the schedule had been rearranged with the idea of working quickly through a series of unanswered questions, he calmly explained, in French as precise and nuanced as Bakkali's, what made him 'turn out like this'. He described a loving, well-off family in Tunisia. A good education, a future marked out for him. And then, at the end of 2010, the fruit seller sets himself on fire, it's the start of the Arab Spring. Immense hopes, tremendous disappointments. Tunisia becomes a breeding ground for jihadists. The Tunisian youths who not so long ago were trying to leave for Europe via Lampedusa on half-inflated Zodiacs are now leaving for Syria. Explaining how he came to join the Islamic State (in 2014, at twenty-one), Ayari evokes a political rather than a religious choice. He could have led a quiet, selfish life on the right side of society, if it weren't for the 'feelings of solidarity and anger' that give the Islamic State 'a certain legitimacy'. He goes to fight in Syria, first against Bashar's troops, then things get more confusing. He's wounded in Homs, four jaw operations. In Raqqa he discovers the chaos. 'When you go to fight, if a fighter falls next to you, you say it was his choice. But when you see people who've never hurt anyone fleeing in panic, their faces marked by humiliation, you feel powerless. The things I felt when I saw that weren't easy to digest, so the day I was told: We're going to need you elsewhere, I went. Nobody forced me.' Ayari won't say who's behind the 'we'. Those familiar with his case think it was Osama Atar, the head of the external operations wing of the Islamic State, and incidentally also the brother of Yassine Atar who's in the box and swears he has nothing to do with all of this. In August 2015, Ayari leaves Syria with Osama Krayem. They spend some time on Leros, then follow the Balkan route to Austria, where they meet up with Salah Abdeslam who brings them to Brussels. Ayari is arrested in Molenbeek at the same time as Abdeslam, on 18 March 2016, after an exchange of gunfire with the police that earns them both twenty years in prison in Belgium. Prodded by the presiding judge, Ayari consents to say that he condemns the attacks, on the condition that the violence on both sides be condemned: that of François Hollande as much as that of Abu Bakr al-Baghdadi. His comrades killed innocent people in France, yes, but the Westerners killed many more in Iraq and Syria, and in a much more cowardly way. Between dropping bombs from a plane without running the slightest risk and killing and braving death, which is more courageous? He acknowledges that he's made bad decisions, without disavowing them. 'The context wasn't conducive to lucidity. Intentions and actions aren't always compatible. But that's not for me to judge.' I've summarised what he said, it was much longer, but everyone was impressed by this confession which was anything but that of a deluded fanatic. As Nadia Mondeguer put it at the end of the hearing: 'He spoke excellently, and what he said was top-notch: I loved it.'

Nadia listens

Because Nadia was there, as she was every day. She immediately understood that Ayari was talking about her, that he was talking *to her*, and many people around her who remembered her testimony understood this as well. When he said, 'That woman reminded me of my mother,' I thought that it was something everyone could say: 'Nadia reminds me of my mother.' This heavy smoker with dishevelled grey hair and a wild and desperate sense of humour, damaged today by the successive deaths of her daughter and her husband but always warm and affectionate, with her door always open, is someone everyone would like to have as their mother, or as their girlfriend's mother. With time we got to know each other. Together with Georges Salines she's become my best friend at the trial, and I've started to visit her from time to time, at her home on Boulevard Voltaire, a stone's throw from La Belle Équipe where her daughter Lamia was shot in the back while she, Nadia, listened to nasheeds on the website of the Arab World Institute. I remembered what she said at the trial, about the days following the attack when she climbed the four floors without a lift to the small flat you enter through the kitchen, with the fridge right next to the door. In the living room, which is in the corner of the building with windows looking over the boulevard, I was struck by a familiar atmosphere. Nadia is Egyptian, her living room is oriental but it could be Russian. A narrow corner bench covered with fabrics and cushions, uncomfortable but welcoming: jumble sale furniture, what my mother's emigrant family called 'Louis the Crate-teenth', a pile of books, overflowing ashtrays, a tablecloth at right angles to the wall covering the table on which thrones a VAIO computer so old that Nadia keeps a small fan pointed at it just to keep it cool, and which she has to shove out of the way to make room for the tea set. The tea is a dusty Egyptian brew that's drunk very sweet, served with a lemon cake she made that day. I sit opposite her, a little to one side, and despite the grief that's never far away I feel good, I could stay for hours, I stay for hours. Still talking about Ayari, she says: 'I couldn't care less that he was talking about me, it was what he said. You know, after I testified, one of Bakkali's lawyers came up to me and said: You didn't only make them listen, you made them think. And when Abrini said: We weren't born with Kalashnikovs, I thought: that answer is for me.'

She calls them 'those kids'.

An old dressing room with mildewed plasterboard walls

The Covid week

After Salah Abdeslam and Ali El Haddad Asufi, it's my turn to come down with Covid and spend a week away from the Palais de Justice. Halfway through the V13 trial it's a forced if not unpleasant holiday, which I take advantage of to leaf through my notebooks from the start. In general it must be said: people whose business it is to attend trials, court reporters by profession or by chance like me, are more fascinated by the culprits than by their victims. We feel sorry for the victims, but it's the culprits whose personalities we try to understand. It's their lives we scrutinise in search of the snag, the mysterious point at which they veered towards lying or crime. With V13, it's the opposite. The five weeks of the plaintiffs' testimony rattled us, devastated us, and almost four months later what remains is their faces laid bare by tragedy. And the defendants? We thought their questioning would be captivating but in fact it's not because they've got nothing to say. Well, nothing . . . It's senseless to say 'nothing', because above all that would indicate that we didn't know how to listen. That we didn't try to understand. That we've forgotten Spinoza's great precept: Do not weep; do not wax indignant. Understand. (Incidentally, the opposite position was held by our prime minister at the time, Manuel Valls, who bristled with righteous indignation regarding the attackers' motives: 'Understanding is already justifying.' I do not agree with Manuel Valls.)

A hypothesis

I'll venture a hypothesis. On the side of the victims, people like you and me, we live in a post-historic world. Our lives, and the lives of those who have died, are individual in nature. These people are individuals to whom we've listened, who've moved us, with whom we've identified. I lamented the passing of Lamia and Lola because they were Lamia and Lola, and because they were Nadia's daughter, Georges's daughter, with their studies, their loves, their preferences, their friends, their parties, everything that made them them, and no one else. It's only in a society that has lost its sense of the collective and of History with a big H that one can be so singular, so reduced to oneself. When you consider these young men in the box who are either keeping quiet because they don't recognise our justice system or reciting a catechism that strikes us as retrograde, you really have to force yourself to be interested in them as individuals. That doesn't mean they're not interesting. It means that what's interesting about them, what interests me in any case, is not played out on the terrain of the individual but on the terrain of History. What interests me is the long historical process that produced this pathological mutation of Islam. I keep coming back to Salah Abdeslam's profound, startling sentence explaining that what's wrong with this trial is that no effort is being made to understand the jihadists. '*It's like reading the last page of a book: what you should do is read the book from the start.*' Well put. And on reflection the same applies to everything: we would certainly better understand Russia's current war on Ukraine if we read that book from the beginning. In the present case, what would count as the beginning? The end of the Ottoman Empire after the First World War, as al-Adnani suggested when he declared that the restoration of the caliphate had put an end to ninety years of humiliation by the West? The retreat of the Ottoman armies from Vienna in 1683? I'm starting to pile up history books, books on Islam, both spiritual and political. By Bernard Lewis, Louis Massignon and Maxime Rodinson, whom I knew as a child because he'd been one of my mother's teachers and was later one of her dearest friends . . . But reading these books from the beginning will have to wait. Until the trial is over. Next autumn. In the meantime I flip through my notebooks: the Belle Équipe notebook, the Bataclan notebook. There are so many stories that I haven't had the space to tell, here's one.

Clarisse at the Bataclan

A sure sign: the sound of computer keys on the press
benches. A new plaintiff approaches the stand and begins
to speak. Fingers hang over the keyboards. Will this one
be *good*? (Such a casting-call attitude is terrible, but how
to escape it?) With some, like Clarisse, you know right
away: after a few sentences the keyboards are clicking
away. Blonde, blue-eyed, trim, with quick, clear speech,
Clarisse is thirty, and was twenty-four at the time. She'd
come to the Bataclan with two friends, because she likes
rock music. And what she likes most about rock concerts is looking at everyone: their faces, the way they
move, their energy. Tonight the energy is excellent.
They're in the pit, on the right, her favourite spot. They're
broke students, alcohol is expensive at the bar, discreetly
they pass around a small flask of whisky but it's empty
in no time, what they need now is some good cold beers.
They decide to go and buy some at the supermarket on
the corner, taking advantage of the fact that the band is
playing a song that they know is long and not very good,
'Kiss the Devil' – many will come back to the title later,
some will also point out that 13 November is World
Kindness Day. The three of them leave the main hall.
Near the cloakroom there's a bouncer who they have to
coax into letting them go out and come back in again.
Clarisse says she just needs to dash out and get some
money from the cashpoint. Whether or not the bouncer

believes her he says okay, then his expression darkens when the first shots ring out. As the danger is coming from outside, Clarisse and her friends rush back in, with the shooters hot on their heels. They manage to return without being killed, but she thinks that's exactly what's going to happen, she's going to be shot in the back, she wonders if she's going to die at once or if she'll suffer. She bursts back into the concert hall, forcing her way through the crowd, pushing and shouting: 'Someone's shooting!' But by now everyone knows that someone's shooting, that it's gunfire and not firecrackers or part of the concert. On the stage she sees the band's singer abandoning his guitar and disappearing into the wings. Everyone throws themselves on the ground, there's shooting, more shooting, they start to hear the screams of those who've been hit. For a moment Clarisse clings to the idea that it's a hostage-taking, if we just do what they ask everything'll be fine, but no, it's not a hostage-taking, these guys have come to kill us all, for no reason, with no discussion possible, there's no point saying we don't agree. She thinks: this is crazy, I'm going to die in a small concert hall where I came to hear a group of nice but not very good Californian rednecks, my ticket cost 30 euros and 70 cents, that is going to be how I die. Everyone jostles, tramples, there's no end of shooting. Someone's turned on the spotlights in the hall, everything is bathed in a blinding white light, worse than the darkness. Clarisse manages to get over to one side. She climbs the stairs, followed in total confusion by fifty or so people. She leads the way, rushing up the stairs in the hope of finding an emergency exit. They hear a huge explosion, she thinks it's a grenade, in fact it's the terrorist Samy Amimour who's blown himself up, showering the pit with a confetti of human flesh. There's a room at the end of the passageway, she pushes open the door: dead end. No windows, no exits. It's an old dressing room with mildewed plasterboard walls, I'm twenty-four, I've got my whole life to live, I'm not going to die in an old dressing room with mildewed plasterboard walls. There's a toilet, a tiny toilet, that's when Clarisse remembers an old James Bond film, *GoldenEye*, where he escapes through the ceiling, so she climbs up on the toilet seat and starts smashing the ceiling with her fists. It's a false ceiling, practically made of cardboard. She rips out the fibreglass insulation and the electrical wires. At the head of the cohort behind her is an older man who could be her father's age, and in fact he looks like her father. He gives her a leg up and she finds herself in crawl space between the false and the real ceiling. The guy and several others follow, they crawl through this narrow passageway amid fibreglass and twisted wires, she wonders if instead of being killed by a bullet she's going to be electrocuted. She crawls, they crawl, finally they reach a ventilation room where they can stand. It's a refuge but it could be a death trap, more and more people are coming and it could lead to them being discovered, maybe the killers will come there and kill them, or the police will throw gas and they'll die of asphyxiation. Clarisse stands next to this man who's her father's age, his name is Patrick, and she asks him to hold her if the killers come. If she has to die, it would be better to die in someone's arms. Patrick promises. The shots continue, in bursts and then one at a time. They can hear people moaning, screaming, dying. Phones ringing. But that's all a long way off, muffled, they're like children in hiding. At the beginning of the trial, the investigator who was one of the first on the scene said he was afraid they could miss some people who'd hidden, only to have them die in their mouse holes. Clarisse, Patrick and the others don't die, but they stay in their mouse hole for a long time, almost four hours, they're the last to be evacuated. They have to be led out through the pit, in the blinding white light. The investigator tells her to close her eyes. Patrick puts his arm around her and his hand over her eyes to stop her from looking, but she looks and will never forget what she sees.

The death convoy

The companion

On 12 November 2015, three hired cars leave Charleroi, in Belgium, at around 5 p.m., and reach Bobigny, in the Parisian suburbs, around eight. The ten members of the commando divide themselves up between the cars according to their personal affinities and the targets they'll hit the next day. Those who'll attack the Bataclan take the Polo, the Iraqis who'll hit the Stade de France drive in the SEAT. Three are in the Clio at the head of the convoy: Brahim and Salah Abdeslam and Mohamed Abrini. Along with Abdelhamid Abaaoud, who's driving the SEAT, the Abdeslam brothers are to blow themselves up after killing as many people as possible on the terraces of several cafés in the 11th arrondissement. And Mohamed Abrini? Nothing is planned for Mohamed Abrini. If he's now in the box next to Salah Abdeslam, it's not because like him he renounced his mission or couldn't activate his suicide belt. And if he was next to him at the head of what he himself called the 'death convoy', it wasn't as a member of the commando but – how to put it? As a companion? Yes, there's no other word for it. Let's take things from the top. Mohamed

Abrini is a childhood friend of Abdeslam's. They grew up together in Molenbeek, where they were inseparable. A small-time multi-offender, he's a regular at Brahim's café Les Béguines, where they watch Islamic State videos – in particular the one featuring his other great friend, Abdelhamid Abaaoud. But he shows no trace of true radicalisation until his younger brother, Souleymane, leaves to get himself killed in Syria. From then on the Quran becomes, in Abrini's own words, his 'only friend'. In June 2015, he too leaves for Syria, to mourn at Souleymane's grave, he says, but also to go to Raqqa to meet up with Abaaoud, who's actively preparing the November attacks. Although it's through the back door, he joins the prestigious brotherhood of those who have been to Syria. Back in Molenbeek, he spends the autumn renting flats and cars, and accompanies Salah Abdeslam to a fireworks shop called Wizards of Fire. Even the trial's order of indictment, which is not very romantic by nature, could not resist making this name the title of a chapter. All of this, taken together, makes Mohamed Abrini the ideal candidate for joining the commando. So why didn't he? Why, apparently, was there never any question of him joining it? Because he simply didn't want to? That's plausible: some people have a vocation for martyrdom, others don't. But then he should have stayed behind. He should have hugged his friends and sent them off with some kind of overblown phrase like: 'See you in heaven, brother.' No: he goes along on the death convoy. They take the trip together. Then, leaving them to kill and die, he returns home. He resurfaces on 22 March 2016, at Brussels-Zaventem Airport, where a surveillance camera shows him pushing a luggage trolley with two guys who will blow themselves up a few minutes later – but this time too, he will not. Other surveillance cameras show him hurrying from the building plunged in chaos. He's wearing a hat, which is why throughout the investigation he'll be known as 'the man in the hat'.

'Let's cut the paranoia'

Surly, resigned and at the same time aggressive, Mohamed Abrini is one of the defendants who on the face of it have nothing to lose. Tried now in France and soon in Belgium for the attack on the airport, he's in for a double max, so no need to make a good impression. He makes strange use of this paradoxical freedom of expression: whereas he's vehement about general ideas, he's evasive regarding the facts – which today have to do with the last months in the run-up to the attacks. But on general ideas, there's no holding him back. Here are a few excerpts: 'You say I'm an extremist, I say that sharia is the divine law, above the law of men. I can understand that people feel sorry for those killed and hurt in the attacks, but they were a response to violence. When you're being killed in Syria, it's normal to come and kill in France.' The execution videos? 'You have to put them in context. It's like young people today who watch series on Netflix. And let's cut the paranoia: there were plenty of videos about school construction, roadwork, helping people in need . . .' The presiding judge, somewhat over-whelmed: 'Still, the beheadings . . .' 'This is nuts: that's all you think about! You do the same thing here: you even beheaded your king!' 'And the systematic rape of Yazidi women, who've been made into sex slaves?' 'You call it rape, I call it a birth programme.' Two hours like that, listening as he tells the court that you really have to have a twisted mind to see only the dark side of the mas-sacre of 131 people. Two hours from which I retain the powerful, dreamlike image of half a dozen bearded men going down into the cellar of Les Béguines café to gather with shining eyes around *videos of schools being built in Raqqa.*

(Still it must be said: videos of school construction in Raqqa did exist. It wasn't only sadists who joined the Islamic State. Some came to build a country, an austere, contemplative society in keeping with the teachings of the Prophet. Reading Hugo Micheron's book, I was star-tled when one young man compares the appeal al-Sham exerts on Arabs to the appeal Israel exerts on Jews. And there were some who did see it that way, in good faith – and some who behaved like settlers, no more tender with the Syrian inhabitants than the Israelis with the Palestinians.)

The copper kettle

In *Jokes and Their Relation to the Unconscious*, Freud tells the story of a man who borrows a copper kettle from another man, and when he gives it back the man sues him because the kettle has a hole in it. His defence: 1) I gave you back the kettle undamaged; 2) The kettle already had a hole in it when I got it from you; 3) I never borrowed a kettle from you at all. Mohamed Abrini uses the same logic the next day when he's asked more precise questions about his return from Syria in the summer of 2015. Once you've crossed the Turkish border, the normal route is Istanbul–Brussels, and in fact he already has the ticket in his pocket. Why, then, does he go through London? Because, he says, Abaaoud asked him to pick up some money that a friend owed him. What friend? What money? Why so many different SIM cards, and why did he spend three days going back and forth between London, Birmingham and Manchester, where he took numerous photos of the stadiums and the train stations? Doesn't that sound like scouting for an attack? 'More paranoia!' Abrini snaps. Why, then, instead of flying from London directly home to Brussels, did he pass through Paris? Why did he ask two friends to pick him up in a car? And why in central Paris, and not at Roissy Airport? Flustered, Abrini lists reasons worthy of Freud's kettle story: 1) I was afraid of being arrested; 2) The ticket was cheaper; 3) We wanted to eat at

McDonald's on the Champs-Élysées; 4) I was afraid they'd get lost (the presiding judge, exasperated: 'It's not as if the way from Roissy to Charles-de-Gaulle Airport weren't marked.'); 5) I have no idea, I don't remember and in any case it's none of your business.

In the Clio

If the truth be told, no one really cares about Mohamed Abrini's zigzag journeys or absurd justifications – at least I don't. What I would like to know, skipping ahead a few months, is what went down inside the Clio during the trip from Charleroi to Bobigny. What these three men – two of whom were intent on dying and the third who wasn't – said to each other. If the two brothers tried to persuade their childhood friend to follow through with them right to the end, to please God and because they were going to blow everything sky-high. If they were serious or if they joked around. If they recited suras or took digs at each other. Who was driving, who was in the back. Unlike so many others, these questions have definite answers. And two of the three passengers, Abrini and Abdeslam, know them. Brahim blew himself up at Le Comptoir Voltaire, but the other two are sitting next to each other in the box. We see them talking in low voices, sometimes sniggering. In a few weeks, when it comes time to reconstruct the facts, will they talk then?

The heart of the heart of the matter

An empty ashtray?

Not since François Hollande's testimony have so many people been present. This is the second interrogation of Salah Abdeslam, devoted to the last months before the attacks – the next will deal with the last days. The time when we made bets on whether or not he'll talk, on the grounds that he'd remained silent throughout the preliminary inquiry, is long over. Not only does he talk, he seems happy to make himself heard, happy to attract so many people. His white shirt is well ironed, he's on good form, the interrogation will last more than seven hours. Polite and obliging on the whole, with a sense of repartee bordering at times on insolence. The presiding judge quotes a letter Salah sent to his mother from prison, in which he states that even if his brother Brahim blew himself up and he didn't, they're both martyrs. Abdeslam interrupts: 'The time hasn't come to talk about that because it gets us to the heart of the matter, and even to the heart of the heart of the matter. I'm not questioning your intellectual capacity, Your Honour, but we shouldn't try to hurry things.' Judge Périès smiles, more amused than offended. One does not get the impression that the heart of the heart of the matter runs as deep as all that. In any case it's no Dostoevskian abyss reeking of the breath of hell. Rather one is struck by the lightness, the inconsistency, the recklessness of this boy whom everyone describes as a nice guy – and maybe he is – but who nevertheless took part in the massacre of 131 people. But is that a reason to agree with his first lawyer, the Belgian Sven Mary, who maintains that his client has a brain like an empty ashtray? I don't think so. He seems more like a sap caught up in his own contradictions: a rigorous Muslim partygoer, a fanatic attached to his cushy life, a cowardly terrorist who assures the court that he pledged allegiance to the Islamic State forty-eight hours before the attacks, no, after the attacks, no, before: we're lost, and no doubt so is he.

The third version

Nothing he says carries much weight, nevertheless one thing he says does resemble a line of defence. It consists of two points. Firstly: 'I didn't kill anyone, I didn't hurt anyone, I have no blood on my hands.' This is true, as it is of all of the accused, since those who did the killing are dead. Secondly: 'I understand that this court wants to set an example. But what will someone who's in the metro with a suitcase containing fifty kilos of explosives say to himself if he thinks better of it at the last moment? What will he do if he thinks that he won't be forgiven anyway, and that he'll be locked up and humiliated like me?' In other words: if there's no incentive to repent *in extremis*, then everyone will blow themselves up. The argument is both shocking and not entirely absurd. If someone who hasn't killed gets as severe a punishment – that is, the maximum – as someone who has, we all feel vaguely that something's wrong. Will this line of reasoning give Salah Abdeslam a chance of getting less, a tiny bit less, than the life sentence everyone assumes is in store for him? Does this slimmest of chances explain his transition from the shady Islamic State fighter he claimed to be at the start of the trial to the immature young punk standing in the box today? Between pride and caution, you might as well choose pride if you're sure you've got nothing to lose. But what if you're not? What if there's a third way? This is the question everyone has been asking themselves from the start: if Salah Abdeslam didn't detonate his suicide belt as planned, is it 1) because it didn't work? 2) because he was afraid? In the first version he's excusable – according to jihadist values. In the second he's pitiful – according to everyone's values. But then out of the blue he slips in a third version: when he saw all these people his age, who looked like him and who like him had put on their best shirt and were laughing and enjoying life on the terraces, he felt a deep empathy and resolved not to go through with it. In this third version it wasn't himself that he spared, but the others. This will forever be unverifiable, but as a defence strategy it's worth a try.

The road trip

In August 2015, Salah Abdeslam went to Greece with his friend Ahmed Dahmani, known as Gégé, on a holiday that would have put Dahmani in the box as well if he weren't already imprisoned in Turkey. Because it was a holiday, Salah and Gégé insist, and you have to have a pretty devious mind to imagine anything else. But that's exactly what Gérard Chemla and Aude Rimailho, both lawyers for the plaintiffs, have. What they think is that this trip was a scouting mission for the route the commando would take from Syria to Belgium two months later. In support of this hypothesis they present, hour by hour, Dahmani's phone-tracking records. Abdeslam's mobile, as if by chance, had remained in Molenbeek and so showed no activity. 30 July, 4.13 p.m. – car rental in Brussels. 31 July, 2.45 a.m. – departure from Brussels. 8.45 a.m. – customs check near Basel. 3.22 p.m. – arrival in Florence. 1 August, 7.30 p.m. – ferry boarding in Bari. 2 August, 1.30 p.m. – arrival in Patras, Greece. 4 August, 6 p.m. – departure from Patras. 5 August, 9.30 a.m. – arrival in Bari. 6 August, 1.25 a.m. – Swiss border. Return to Brussels at 8.30 a.m. When this itinerary is read out in court, its effect is both comical and damning. What's the point of this whirlwind tour if they didn't see a thing? Abdeslam: 'We had some time on our hands, a bit of money, we went on a road trip, it had nothing to do with the Islamic State.' 'But what did you do? What did you do when you stopped?' 'We ate pasta, visited some islands.' 'What islands?' 'I can't remember their names.' 'Still,' says Judge Périès, 'you travel two days in one direction, then two days in the other, to stay just two days at your destination, it's a bit strange . . .' 'A bit strange . . . No doubt you can afford more luxurious holidays, Your Honour, but we can't.' I report this little exchange not because it's so important in itself, but because it well illustrates the perpetual change of perspective during a trial. When I listen to the plaintiffs' lawyers, this journey strikes me as extremely fishy: a road trip, what a joke. Then the defence speaks. What does Abdeslam's lawyer Olivia Ronen say? First of all, that this isn't the route the terrorists took two months later. Secondly, there's nothing stopping two young guys from Molenbeek from crossing Europe non-stop with the music blasting, their foot to the floor while smoking joint after joint, just for the fun of it. And it's wrong to conclude that their aims had to be criminal just because they didn't stop in at the Uffizi Galleries when they passed through Florence as the presiding judge and his assistants would have done. Listening to her I think: true. Just as there's nothing stopping Abdeslam from deciding not to blow himself up out of pure altruism.

(But then I think: okay, but if it was true, why didn't they say so earlier?)

The logistics of terror

Abdeslam drives

After the last months, the last weeks. On 24 August 2015 at 7 p.m., Salah Abdeslam went to the Rent a Car agency at 178 Chaussée de Haecht in the Brussels suburb of Haren. There he rented a BMW 118d, registration number 1-HXV990. He was accompanied by Mohamed Abrini, whose mobile number he left along with his own, and who will in fact receive a call from the agency on 31 August, the scheduled return date, and then again on 5 September, the actual return date. After the rental there's no sign of the vehicle until 29 August, when it's fined on the Rue Paul Delvaux in Brussels at 3.10 a.m. On 30 August at 3.40 p.m., it enters Hungary at the Hegyeshalom border crossing. It's flashed for speeding at 4.27 p.m. near Tatabánya. At 4.50 it's in Biatorbágy, and at 6.29 it reaches the small town of Kiskőrös, 130 kilometres south of Budapest. At 8.40 the car passes through Biatorbágy again, where it had been almost three hours earlier. The return journey ends in Brussels in the late afternoon of 1 September. What's more, between 30 August at 0.58 a.m. and 1 September at 10.53 p.m. – that is between the start and the end of his journey as reconstructed by the motorway and telephony data – Salah Abdeslam's usual mobile line is tracked to his home in Molenbeek, without making or receiving any calls. That means he left his phone there, as he did during his road trip to Greece three weeks earlier. When asked about this, he'll say that it's normal when you go away to want to have some peace. However, during the whole trip he uses another Belgian line, which makes frequent calls to two Hungarian numbers. The Hungarian SIM cards were bought on 27 August in a phone shop at a supermarket in Kiskőrös. The saleswoman, Dorina Petrovics, identified the two individuals to whom she sold the cards as Bilal Hadfi and Chakib Akrouh. The first will blow himself up at the Stade de France, the second will be part of the commando that attacks the terraces, together with Brahim Abdeslam and Abdelhamid Abaaoud, and will blow himself up five days later. Their journey can also be reconstructed. Arriving from Syria, they travel through Turkey and Greece and arrive in Serbia on 24 August. From that date, they communicate first with an unidentified Syrian-based contact, then with a Belgian-based coordinator who is most certainly Khalid el-Bakraoui – who will later kill himself in the 2016 Brussels metro bombing – and finally, from 29 August, with the driver of the BMW, Salah Abdeslam. They arrive in Budapest on 27 August and travel to Kiskőrös, where they spend their nights in the forest opposite the train station. 'Tell the guys to send a message when they're in front of the station so we can come out quickly. Tell them the password,' Chakib Akrouh says to the Syrian contact. The contact passes the information to Khalid el-Bakraoui, and tells Akrouh that the driver will need a day, maybe a day and a half, to make it there. This is how Salah Abdeslam, who'd rented the car on 24 August so as to be ready, one assumes, when he gets the green light, sets off on the night of 29 August and returns with his two passengers on the evening of 1 September. It's not known who meets them in Brussels when Abdeslam drops them off, or in which hideout they'll stay – details which are known with precision, however, for the next arrivals.

Wizards of fire

This data is tedious. I've quoted just a tiny sample to give an idea of the kind of things contained in the 542-volume legal brief that are now being detailed to the court, hearing after hearing. To summarise: at the end of August and start of September 2015, twelve Islamic State fighters, coming from Syria and posing as Syrian refugees, entered Europe through the Balkan route. Salah Abdeslam went to pick them up in five separate trips to Hungary and Germany and brought them back to Belgium, where they were split up between five hideouts rented by Mohamed Bakkali. Posing as one of two IT specialist aliases, either Fernando Castillo or Alberto Malonzo, he was dressed in a suit and tie with a curly wig and huge glasses, which did not prevent the owner of one of the flats from finding the fake Malonzo 'quite classy'. The terrorists were all provided with Belgian identity cards by a network known as the 'Catalogue', through an intermediary named Farid Kharkhach. Kharkhach is in the box today and never stops repeating that he may be a forger and petty criminal, but he had no idea what he was getting himself into. Leaving aside the weapons, which are a blind spot in the case because it's still not known where the six Kalashnikovs used in the attacks came from, each person's role in the logistical preparations seems clear. Bakkali was responsible for the hideouts, Abdeslam for transportation. At times their roles blurred, however. That's how it happened that, after picking up Bilal Hadfi and Chakib Akrouh in Hungary and before returning the BMW to the Rent a Car agency in Haren, Abdeslam drove to the fireworks shop Wizards of Fire, situated at 21 Avenue de la Mare in Saint-Ouen-l'Aumône, near Paris, in the early afternoon of 4 September. There he bought a wood-and-aluminium case containing twelve receiver boxes and a remote firing system that can send an electric impulse four hundred metres. The salesman, Valentin Lithare, found this purchase of remote firing equipment without accompanying fireworks very unusual, but the customer paid 390 euros in cash and after all it was his right. Abdeslam entered the shop alone, but the phone records suggest that he was accompanied by Mohamed Abrini, who stayed in the car. It was once again accompanied by Abrini – this time for sure – that on 8 October, on his way back from Vienna where he'd picked up Osama Krayem, Sofien Ayari and the explosives expert Ahmad Alkhald, Abdeslam drove another BMW to two Irrijardin shops near Beauvais in northern France, to buy chemicals for balancing swimming-pool water. The manager of the first shop, Madame Allard, recalls that the two men wanted only Bayroshock canisters, and that she was unable to help them because she finds Bayroshock too expensive and stocks only the cheaper Irripool brand. They had better luck with Monsieur Demaiter, the manager of the second shop and exclusive Bayroshock dealer. He was surprised that the men wanted to buy as many canisters as possible, because half of one is more than enough for any home swimming pool, but he was able to sell them three – more than they needed to make the TATP used in the attacks. Bayroshock or nothing, Ahmad Alkhald apparently demanded, and he wasn't kidding about the quality.

A terrific pain in the arse

When asked about these items, Salah Abdeslam said he just wanted 'to set off fireworks'. About his travels, he said he'd gone to look for 'brothers in Islam', political refugees fleeing the war, the way Ukrainians are fleeing Russia's bombs today, and the way the Jews fled the Nazi persecutions of the past. He seems not to have grasped that such references could rub people up the wrong way. He refused to name the person whose orders he was following, most likely Khalid el-Bakraoui, on the grounds that he was not going to rat on a brother. To finish, he complained that the judicial system had 'broken' his life, provoking a case of disrespectful behaviour when a burst of ironic applause came from the plaintiffs' benches. Judge Périès did not pick up on it – although he should have, because, while understandable, such reactions are not permitted. The defence lawyers rose as one and stormed out in protest. The next day everything was back to normal. There were times during this trial when the main defendant made a less bad impression than others. It seems like a trifling shortcoming in relation to what he's charged with, but on top of everything else, this week he came across as a terrific pain in the arse.

The countdown

The computer on the Rue Max Roos

On 22 March 2016, a Bruxelles Propreté bin lorry makes its morning rounds. In a rubbish bin on the Rue Max Roos in the Schaerbeek district, the bin men find two computers, a tablet and a mobile phone. A stroke of luck, except that one of the computers is completely broken with half the keys ripped out: good for the dump. The tablet and phone are in no better condition, but when the other computer, a black Hewlett-Packard PC, is turned on, the desktop shows seven hooded men posing in front of an Islamic State flag. It's not known whether the bin men immediately identified the Islamic State flag, as it's not them testifying but one of our old friends the Belgian investigators. Within the hour they learn, along with everyone else in Brussels, that two suicide bombers have just blown themselves up at Brussels-Zaventem Airport, while a third has blown himself up at Maelbeek metro station. Thirty-two dead, 340 injured, the deadliest attacks ever committed in Belgium. The bin men bring the computer to the police, who've already discovered the identity of the terrorists, all of whom were also involved in the 13 November attacks. In the metro station: Khalid el-Bakraoui. At the airport: Ibrahim el-Bakraoui and Najim Laachraoui, together with the eternal companion Mohamed Abrini who, as four months earlier in Paris, prudently slips away under his bucket hat while his buddies set off their suicide belts. All of this is only alluded to at V13 because it will be the subject of another trial set to take place this autumn in Belgium, where Abdeslam, Abrini, etc. will also appear and which must not be anticipated here. The computer discovered in the bin, however, is of great interest to the court. The terrorists tossed it out on the morning of the attack when they left their hideout in the Rue Max Roos. They'd deleted most of the files the day before, so the contents can't be retrieved. But the Belgian police geeks have managed to reconstruct its activity history, and here's what it tells us: The computer was put into service on 14 August 2015. On 12 October, a folder called *Moutafajirat* ('Explosives') and more importantly one called *Targets* were created. Clearly it's around this time that the project is taking shape. Among the targets being considered are *Jeunesse Catholique / Royalistes / Civitas* (Civitas is a royalist fundamentalist Catholic movement), *Punks* and *Défense* (the Défense business district in Paris? The Ministry of Defence?). If the attackers had stuck to these targets, the attacks would have aroused a very different set of emotions. Imagine if the victims had been fundamentalist Catholics, mowed down as they left Saint-Nicolas-du-Chardonnet church – the hotspot of French traditionalist Catholicism – or punk rockers with their dogs, shot in their hangout in the basement of the Forum des Halles: yes, their deaths would have been mourned, but the thirty-somethings drinking mojitos on the café terraces while puffing on their vapes wouldn't have identified with them nearly as much. Less than a month later, things were narrowed down further: on 7 November the *13 November* folder was created. It contains five subfolders: *Omar Group* (the terrace commando led by Abdelhamid Abaaoud, alias Abu Omar); *Iraqi Group* (the Stade de France commando); *French Group* (containing a file named *Virtual visit of the Bataclan* intended for band managers), *Schiphol Group* (named after Schiphol Airport in Amsterdam), and finally *Metro Group*. They've narrowed the targets down, but are still groping. They toss around the idea of an attack on the Paris metro but nothing comes of that, and then on Schiphol Airport, which won't happen either. 7 November–13 November: the closeness of these dates is enough to make your head spin. Six days before the attacks, everything was still open. There was going to be an attack, but at that point the targets could still have been very different. The young people who'd bought their tickets for the Eagles of Death Metal might have come out of the Bataclan after the concert to learn that a massacre had just taken place at Châtelet-Les Halles metro station. They would have been horrified, and worried sick about their friends who might have been there around that time, and then they'd have gone home. At that hearing I was sitting next to Georges Salines. Our eyes met, I knew what he was thinking: other people would have died, Lola would still be alive.

The Virtuous Scoundrel

The computer's activity reveals other mysteries. The films viewed include not only the Islamic State's bloodthirsty propaganda videos, but also a recording of a stage production of *Cyrano de Bergerac*, Robert Hossein's adaptation of *Les Misérables*, and above all two comedies by Sacha Guitry, *Royal Affairs in Versailles* and *The Virtuous Scoundrel*. I have no idea what kind of films the Abdeslam brothers or Mohamed Abrini may like, and I may be wrong in thinking that above all they watch American blockbusters, but black-and-white films by Sacha Guitry shot in the 1950s, with dated language and crackling sound? No way. I watched *The Virtuous Scoundrel*, just to be sure. Who knows, maybe it would reveal some small echo, some detail that can connect two such radically different universes as those of a Belgian jihadist and a witty, flamboyant man of the theatre, the supremely uninhibited representative of a world that has long since sunk into oblivion. There are none. *The Virtuous Scoundrel* tells the story of a rich and respectable man, brilliantly played by Michel Simon, and his bohemian brother, also brilliantly played by Michel Simon. They're twins, one of them dies, the other takes his place: it's a black comedy, very funny, I recommend it. The idea that our jihadists could have watched this film between two beheading videos in the cellar of the café Les Béguines was evoked in passing as a strange idea not worth dwelling on. Only one lawyer for the plaintiffs found it, as I did, bizarre enough to try to search for an explanation: perhaps, she conjectured, it was under these headings that the jihadists hid their most compromising files? Good try, but that explanation only replaces one conundrum with another. It's hard enough to believe that these guys watched Sacha Guitry films a few days before the attacks, but that they code-named their recipes for explosives or lists of hideouts after them . . .

Cans of Oasis and a packet of frangipane biscuits

Day by day we get closer to 13 November, and things become ever more dark and oppressive. 8 November: cash deposits and withdrawals, 2,500 euros. 9 November: Abrini, the Abdeslam brothers and the second fiddle Mohammed Amri rent the Clio, the Polo and the SEAT. 10 November: they rent the hideouts in the Paris suburbs of Bobigny and Alfortville. 11 November: activation of the fourteen telephone lines that establish permanent contact between the 'coordinators' in Belgium – most probably the el-Bakraoui brothers – and those whom the Belgian investigator calls 'the authors' – yes, that's the term, the 'authors' of the crime. 12 November: the 'death convoy' sets off. The Iraqis who'll hit the Stade de France are with Abaaoud in the SEAT, the Abdeslam brothers and Abrini take the Clio, and the three assigned to the Bataclan are with Hadfi in the Polo, which stops from 3.36 to 3.41 p.m. at the Total station in Nivelles. A surveillance camera films them in the shop: three young guys in light jackets and trainers buying cans of Tropical Oasis fruit drink and a packet of frangipane biscuits. They laugh. They know they'll be dead the next evening, but they'll have killed a lot of people before they die. As many as possible. How many would that be? Did they make predictions as they drove? Did they make bets? If they'd been told: tomorrow you'll have killed ninety people, would they have found that a) better than expected? b) so-so? c) a little on the disappointing side?

Mohamed Abrini drops his mask

Mixed up in his mind

After the last weeks, the last days. The last hours. Rivals in the art of suspense, Mohamed Abrini and Salah Abdeslam have both announced that they will disclose key information when we finally get to 13 November and, after kilometres of motorway and telephony data, surveillance cameras and Belgian investigators, we're here. Abrini has put on a white shirt to mark the occasion. When Judge Périès is lenient and allows him to remove his mask, he exclaims: 'You're right, Your Honour: let's drop our masks!' Then in a theatrical tone very unlike him, he continues: 'We all wear masks, but sometimes it's hard to take them off without removing some of our own skin' – a sentence that a quick collective search attributes to Quebec novelist André Berthiaume: the jihadists' references never cease to amaze. Abrini's disclosure boils down to this one sentence: 'I was to be part of the operation on the 13th.' In other words: I wasn't the simple companion I claimed to be throughout the investigation, someone who was just along for the ride to bid farewell to my friends. No, I was meant to blow myself up along with the rest. So why didn't he? It's here that things become confused. Let's take them from the top. In September, Abrini has a meeting in Charleroi with Abdelhamid Abaaoud, who's come back from Syria under cover and is busy preparing the attacks. Without going into details or specifying where and when it will happen, Abaaoud tells Abrini that he's counting on his participation. Ever since they were teenagers Abaaoud has exerted a huge influence on Abrini, as he has on all the petty delinquents at Les Béguines. For Abrini, saying no and 'going head to head' with Abaaoud is out of the question. So? 'So I don't say yes, I don't say no. I don't say anything.' Then in the weeks that follow he acts as if the conversation had never taken place. Abrini works at the Délinice Halal deli in Molenbeek. He's preparing his wedding – there's been no mention of this so far, but this man who's preparing to blow himself up in public is also about to get married. Deep down he knows that he could never kill random people in the street and then blow himself up. But – still so as not to disappoint Abaaoud – he doesn't dare to come out and say so, and helps Salah Abdeslam with the preparation: renting cars and hideouts, buying chemicals and remote firing equipment. 'All of this openly and without taking the slightest precaution?' the prosecution asks. 'Like someone for whom it doesn't really matter one way or the other because he knows he's going to die anyway? Because you knew you were going to die?' 'Yes, well,' he says, 'I knew without knowing, it wasn't clear to me, things were mixed up in my mind, I was hoping to go under the radar.' On 10 November he still thought they were all going to Paris to go shopping, he says. It was only on the 11th that he realised that no, 'all hell was going to break loose and we'd get blown to smithereens'. We arrive at 12 November and the infamous 'death convoy'. What went down inside the Clio in which Abrini was travelling with the two Abdeslam brothers? This is perhaps what intrigues me the most about this whole sequence of events. 'How would you describe the atmosphere in the car?' he's asked. 'Would you say it was good?' 'Uh, it was calm. Brahim played a CD with nasheeds . . .' 'And you told him you weren't going to be in on it?' Here Abrini gets muddled. He can't remember, things are mixed up in his mind. But there must have been one moment when he said to someone – Abaaoud? Brahim? – that he wasn't going to go through with it. Either that, or right up until the last minute he didn't dare to come clean. But if that's the case, how to reconcile it with the most surprising of his disclosures: unlike him, Salah was not meant to take part in the attacks? Because it was also only at the last minute that Salah was ordered – by whom? Abaaoud? Brahim? – to take the suicide belt left empty by Abrini's defection. At this moment all eyes are fixed on Abdeslam: he knows whether this is true or not. Will he confirm it tomorrow? Suspense. The death convoy arrives in Bobigny. Is that when Abrini spoke out? If so, how did Brahim take it? Has he already designated his younger brother as Abrini's replacement, and in that case, how did his brother react? Nothing is clear, things are still mixed up in Abrini's mind. Everything happens like in a dream. He'd like to backtrack, but he can only go forward. They're all together in the hideout, a house in Bobigny he'd rented with Brahim the day before. The cars have been unloaded, the Kalashnikovs and suicide belts are lined up against a wall like gardening equipment. Is that when Abrini talked? To whom? He doesn't remember. Nor does he remember what time he left the house. It was late – in any event he goes out alone. He walks to Noisy-le-Sec, a few kilometres away, where he eats in a pizzeria. At midnight he calls a taxi to take him to the station so he can take a train back to Brussels. The most plausible explanation for this totally erratic behaviour is that he didn't dare say anything to anyone, and used any pretext – going out for a smoke – to flee as if he had all the devils of hell on his heels. This is confirmed by what follows: as only to be expected, there is no train from Noisy-le-Sec to Brussels at midnight, so instead of taking a room at the nearest cheap hotel, Abrini persuades the taxi driver to accept 450 euros for a ride to Brussels, where he arrives at 4 a.m. He pays 300 euros in cash, gets the driver to drop him off near a bar where he says he can get the missing 150 euros, and leaves the driver high and dry. Then there's a blank. On the afternoon of Friday the 13th he signs the lease, reads the meters, pays the deposit and receives the keys of a new flat, together with his fiancée. This visit to the flat, entirely decoupled from reality, could be straight out of Dostoevsky. Things were no less mixed up, I'm inclined to think, in the mind of the student Raskolnikov after he murdered the old usurer, and Raskolnikov's answers to chief investigator Porfiry Petrovich no more coherent. It's not known where Abrini is when news of the Paris attacks breaks, he doesn't seem to know very well himself. What is known is that he'll spend the next four months going from hideout to hideout. 'I felt trapped,' he'll say. 'I didn't want to take part in the attacks, but I didn't want to leave either. The others talked, I spent the days in a total fog, smoking weed and playing PlayStation.' He resurfaces on 22 March, wearing a hat and pushing a luggage trolley at Brussels-Zaventem airport together with Najim Laachraoui and Ibrahim el-Bakraoui, who are about to blow themselves up. And Abrini? This time too he'll flee at the last minute.

'Not out of cowardice . . .'

The next day it's Abdeslam's turn. Only he can confirm or deny Abrini's statements. Expectations run high. And then a turn of events: today he will make use of his right to silence. Take it or leave it, he doesn't have to justify himself. Judge Périès is at a loss and insists. To no avail. Everyone insists. To no avail. Then at the end of the hearing Claire Josserand-Schmidt, a lawyer for the plaintiffs, appeals to his good nature with such passion and kindness that he agrees to talk about his fiancée, Yasmina, whom he took to dinner on the 10th. He feels bad for making her cry when he told her that he had to go away, perhaps for a long time. Then he talks about the explosive belt that he decided not to activate, 'not out of cowardice, not out of fear, but because I didn't want to', and which he was careful to defuse before throwing it into a dustbin to prevent women or children from detonating it by accident. His answers are selective, and all to his advantage. Until now in this trial the prosecution has always expressed itself in moderate, measured terms. Now, however, public prosecutor Nicolas Le Bris says with cold anger: 'Salah Abdeslam had promised to give us explanations, and he has not. Instead he acts like some kind of a star, teasing the court and clamming up to revel in the reactions he provokes. You do not have an ounce of courage in your body, Mr Abdeslam: this is pure cowardice.' I agree, but that doesn't answer the question: now that he's become so fond of talking, what is it that he doesn't want to say?

Abdelhamid Abaaoud's orange trainers

The conspiracy bush

The three at the Stade de France are the first to blow themselves up. Almost at the same time, the three at the Bataclan go into action. Those assigned to the terraces are less organised. Assuming he was with them at all, Salah Abdeslam has disappeared. His brother Brahim blows himself up at Le Comptoir Voltaire. The leader of the commando Abdelhamid Abaaoud and his vassal Chakib Akrouh remain in the SEAT. Their journey has been reconstructed, from the house in Bobigny to the Place de la République in central eastern Paris: a direct, logical route, a GPS route. From there it's a bloodbath: four stages, twelve minutes, thirty-nine dead. And from then on everything is strangely erratic. The SEAT circles the Place de la Nation three times and takes one-way streets the wrong way: it's hard to make head or tail of what's going on. Finally the two men abandon the car on the other side of the Boulevard Périphérique, in the suburb of Montreuil. Three Kalashnikovs, several magazines and finely sharpened butcher's knives were found in the boot, enough to keep the party going for a while, but they leave it all behind and take the metro at

Croix de Chavaux station. A surveillance camera shows them jumping over the turnstiles, like the harmless free-loaders you let go through behind you with an indulgent smile. The video clearly shows Abaaoud's bright orange trainers: they'll play a key role in what follows. The two then disappear for a while, only to resurface in the suburb of Aubervilliers, on an embankment below the A86 motorway that the police, in their police jargon, will call 'the conspiracy bush'.

Nadia below the motorway

'I can't imagine what that bush is like,' Nadia Mondeguer said to me during the hearing on Abaaoud's last days. 'I'd like to go and see it.' We were sitting next to each other on the plaintiffs' benches. Yann Revol was also there, a young man who was at Le Petit Cambodge and who comes every day. I say 'young man' even though he's forty-six and has grey hair, because he's svelte, he looks young and exudes a gentle warmth. He's a photographer, I found his testimony simple and serious, last autumn he became one of my friends among the V13 regulars. 'Why don't we go together?' I suggested, and we arranged to meet up the following Sunday afternoon. That was 10 April 2022, the first round of the French presidential elections. I came by Nadia's place on Boulevard Voltaire, and we first took a taxi to the Porte des Lilas and from there the 170 bus, because she wanted to get there gradually and not just be dropped off. From Porte des Lilas to Pont du Chemin de Fer in Aubervilliers there are about fifteen stops, but the bus had to take so many detours that we were afraid of missing ours. Pont du Chemin de Fer is the closest stop to 2 Rue des Bergeries, the conspiracy bush's official address. We entered it into our phones, but that didn't stop us from getting lost. The only indications we'd gathered from the testimonies two days earlier were that there's first one roundabout and then another, but in fact there's nothing but round-abouts in this area, and wherever you go you only get to another roundabout. It's an urban wasteland, with barbed wire, puddles, tags on breeze-block walls and halal meat warehouses. No cars, no pedestrians and even, behind the fences, no houses. Nadia and I walk in the sunshine, we talk about what the weather was like between 14 and 17 November 2015. On the 13th it was unusually good for the time of year, she says, that's why so many people were out on the terraces, but then it got worse: sleeping out in the rough for three nights like Abaaoud and Akrouh did was certainly no picnic. Just when we start to think we'll never find it we come to a new round-about, in the middle of which Yann is waiting for us. This is it, he says, this is where the sandwich truck was. Nadia nods: yeah, the sandwich truck. This sandwich truck doesn't ring any bells with me, just like it didn't ring any bells when Nadia talked about 'Tarral' on the bus. She could see I wasn't following and said, a little piqued: 'Rue Georges-Tarral, the hideout in Bobigny!'

Like many of the plaintiffs, Nadia and Yann have an impressive knowledge of the ins and outs of the case. They know everything, you'd think they were speaking in code. Yann had arrived at the La Courneuve-Aubervilliers station, where we think Abaaoud and Akrouh got off, and without a moment's hesitation he leads us to a second roundabout, where the Rue des Bergeries starts. It's there, at this precise spot in this industrial zone, that Hasna and Sonia came to meet Abaaoud and Akrouh. To our left, a fenced-in vacant lot. In the distance, a hypermarket warehouse and a car park with lorries all white and shimmering in the sun. To our right, the embankment below the A86 motorway. I'd imagined a bare embankment like the ones where the migrants camp at the entrances to Paris, but it's not like that at all. This embankment is very steep, with heaps of undergrowth. It's in this little jungle that the conspiracy bush is located. But is that really the right word? Shouldn't it be called the conspiracy thicket, the conspiracy tangle? Nadia sits on a concrete block to smoke a cigarette while Yann and I climb up the embankment. It's muddy and very steep. Even on a dry day like today it's slippery, I can only imagine what it must have been like on a November night in the rain. We grab on to the branches. Halfway up there's a sort of flat area where shredded bin bags, old foam mattresses and the usual rubbish of beer cans, cigarette packets and pizza boxes indicate a recent homeless camp. Nadia calls from down below: is this the place? We go back down and say yes, this has got to be it. She crushes her cigarette in a small metal box full of ashes and fag ends, and shakes her head: this does not add up. Something here does not tally. Yann agrees, and I agree with them. There's a mystery here. Why does Europe's most wanted terrorist, after abandoning an arsenal with which he could have slaughtered at least a few dozen more *kuffar*, end up in such an unlikely place? So hard to get to, so precarious, so uncomfortable? Can it be that nothing had been planned, that there was neither a plan A nor a plan B to organise his escape? A clown like Salah Abdeslam found accomplices to exfiltrate him – we'll discuss that next week – while he, the leader of the commando, the great Abu Omar, winds up here? Reduced to calling someone as pathetic and unreliable as his cousin Hasna Aït Boulahcen for help?

Hasna and Sonia

Abaaoud's cousin Hasna is a 26-year-old girl who's seriously confused and more or less radicalised, although her radicalisation consists of wearing the niqab while getting drunk on Red Bull vodka, smoking joints from morning to night, sleeping with anyone who'll have her and posting pictures of herself naked in a bubble bath on Facebook. For the moment she's crashing at her friend Sonia's flat in Saint-Denis. Sonia's a mother of three who works as a volunteer at the food charity organisation Les Restos du Cœur and takes in, literally and figuratively, all the stray cats in the neighbourhood. On the evening of the attacks, they argue. Hasna says it's normal to kill *kuffar* if you're a good Muslim. Stop talking nonsense, Sonia says, without taking her too seriously. On Sunday, Hasna tells Sonia that she's got a distant cousin who's seventeen and homeless: maybe they could help him out? Of course, says Sonia, who never refuses to help anyone, and they set off in the car towards Aubervilliers, guided on the phone by the cousin because the place is hard to find. The paper chase ends at the deserted roundabout where Nadia and I met up with Yann, and where the sandwich truck was parked at the time. From there the two women follow the Rue des Bergeries to the second roundabout, as we've just done. There they get out of the car. A movement in the bushes, branches rustling, the cousin comes down the embankment in his orange trainers. He's very small, and is dressed in a big bomber jacket and a bucket hat. He looks, Sonia remembers, like the Romanians who take advantage of the backed-up traffic at Porte de la Chapelle to wash your car window whether you like it or not in the hope of scoring 50 cents. One thing is certain, he's not seventeen at all, more like thirty-five. He shakes hands with Sonia, who finds it increasingly difficult to figure out what's going on until, growing suspicious, she asks him if he's got anything to do with the attacks. 'Yes, sister,' the cousin says, 'I won't lie because Allah doesn't like lies. The terraces in the 10th arrondissement, that was me.' He looks very pleased with himself, Hasna beams with pride. After a moment of disbelief, Sonia says that it's horrible to kill innocent people, that it's the opposite of Islam. He gets angry and says that there are worse things than *kuffar*, namely false Muslims like her, and that he has every intention of finishing the work he started. Soon it'll be Christmas, he's going to hit department stores, schools, places where there are Jews . . . ninety brothers will be joining him, it's going to be huge. Bang! Bang! Bang! Hasna and Sonia leave, the first having promised to find her cousin a place to stay, the second devastated and at a complete loss as to what to do next. Back home, she washes the hand that shook Abaaoud's with bleach. Seven years later she still does it sometimes, she says. She doesn't sleep all night. The next morning, Monday the 16th, the two women are watching the images of the massacre the TV has been showing non-stop for three days. Suddenly the face of Hasna's cousin appears, presented as the mastermind of the attacks. He's thought to have orchestrated everything from Syria. But they know that he's not in Syria at all, that he's with a friend in a bivouac on the Rue des Bergeries below the A86 motorway. Hasna's pride is at its peak: her cousin is on TV. Honour to the family. In a general way, Hasna considers that everything that's happened in the last few days has taken place on TV, without any clear connection to real life. Sonia tries to reason with her: the two guys are waiting for accomplices, they're preparing a new attack, if we do nothing dozens of innocent people will die. We have no choice, we have to call the police. Hasna looks at her in horror and swears to Allah that her cousin is a hero, the *kuffar* deserved what they got, and anyway, you don't rat on your own. Sonia waits for Hasna to leave then calls the toll-free number set up after the attacks. She's passed from one service to another in the blurred hierarchy of callers, she's the 2,476th that day and wouldn't be taken seriously if she didn't mention the cousin's orange trainers – the ones shown in the metro video but of which there's been no mention in the media yet. Sonia gives Hasna's number, which is then tapped. The police go into overdrive.

'Because of what's been going on'

Everything Hasna Aït Boulahcen did on her phone in the last two days of her life was recorded and is on file. It's a mind-blowing document that can be read in full in Marc Weitzmann's book *Hate: The Rising Tide of Anti-Semitism in France (and What It Means for Us)** – one of the best books ever written on jihadism. Between Bobigny, where she lives, Aubervilliers, where she goes to meet her cousin, and Saint-Denis, where she's about to die, Hasna wanders from fast-food joint to shopping mall, rambles meaninglessly and bangs against her surroundings like a

---

* Marc Weitzmann, *Hate: The Rising Tide of Anti-Semitism in France (and What It Means for Us)*, Houghton Mifflin Harcourt, 2019.

drunken wasp in a glass. Clinging to her phone, she looks
for 1) hash; 2) suits for Abaaoud and Akrouh to wear at
La Défense business district, where they intend to blow
themselves up at the weekend; 3) a hideout. She buys the
hash but loses a brick along the way and bursts into tears.
As far as the suits go, there's no indication that she went
looking for them at all. Regarding the hideout she has
better luck: her dealer puts her in touch with a certain
Jawad Bendaoud, a dealer himself but also a slumlord in
Saint-Denis, where he rents her a flat in a squat located at
8 Rue du Corbillon, entry code A1218, for 150 euros a
month. She does all of this drunk and stoned and doesn't
really know what it's all about, but no one around her
knows any more than she does. At one point there's a
crazy dialogue with her social worker who calls to help
with her – totally fruitless – search for a job and a place
to live. The call bugs her because, as she says: 'I've drunk
too much and haven't slept. I saw my cousin, he was on
TV.' 'Oh, because of what's been going on?' 'Yeah. He's
wanted, he was on TV. And now I'm in shock, in fact I
don't feel good.' The caller says okay, and moves on to
what he was calling about: a temp job in a fast-food restaurant, she should call them on Monday. Talk to you on
Monday, then. A girl he knows to be unstable and radicalised says she saw her cousin who's wanted 'because of
what's been going on' – i.e. the deadliest attacks in French
history – on TV, and the social worker doesn't react. He
hangs up. Not like Sonia, that's for sure. Sonia knows full
well that in calling the police and denouncing the cousin

who was on TV she may well have signed her own death
warrant.

The Rue du Corbillon

What I don't understand, says Nadia, is not only that
the two guys wound up in that bush, but also that the
police did nothing although they knew exactly where they
were. Here. Right where we are now, on the corner of
the Rue des Bergeries and the Rue Marcel Carné. A place
that's monitored by two surveillance cameras. It would
have been straightforward to catch them: no houses, no
one around, it's deserted. With the noise of the motorway you wouldn't hear the shots. Maybe they could even
have taken them alive: the trial would be very different if
Abaaoud were in the box. But no, they look on without
lifting a finger from 10 p.m. on Monday the 16th until 8
p.m. the next day. The cameras film Hasna coming to
meet them on Tuesday evening and show them emerging from the bush. Abaaoud's orange trainers are clearly
visible. The three of them walk to the sandwich truck
that was on the first roundabout at the time. Hasna calls
a taxi, they wait, the taxi doesn't show. She asks a guy
who's eating a sandwich if he can drive them to a place
in Saint-Denis, not far from there. The guy turns out to
be an Uber driver and says sure, for 20 euros. When they
get there they say they only have 10, so like the taxi driver
who took Abrini to Brussels he'll have to make do with

that. Why did the police wait? They'll say they were afraid there could be more of them, and that they could escape if they closed in when they were outside. Trapping them inside would be better. So they waited until the three had settled in on the Rue du Corbillon, and it was only at 4 in the morning that the anti-terrorist police force launched the assault. The people who lived in the building were scarred for life. The ninjas broke down their doors, handcuffed them, twisted their arms and smashed their teeth just in case they were terrorists, without wasting a word on why. Five thousand rounds of ammunition were fired – all by the police, who were convinced that Abaaoud and Akrouh were sitting on an arsenal, whereas apart from the explosive belt, all they had was a small handgun. The hail of bullets was worsened by the fact that the seventy police officers mistook their own gunshots for enemy fire. The raid lasted for seven hours. At one point Hasna was heard shouting: 'Monsieur, can I come out? Please, monsieur, let me come out!' Right up until the end she had no idea what was going on. Then Akrouh blew himself up, killing Abaaoud and Hasna as well. In the morning the building was reminiscent of Grozny, as people said in those days, today one would say of Mariupol. The assault was followed live from dawn to midday by dozens of French and foreign TV crews. Kids from the neighbourhood set up a small street market to sell videos they'd shot with their phones to journalists who arrived late. The images showed practically nothing, but still they were broadcast non-stop on practically all the channels for at least a couple of days.

Under the radar

The media found a comic counterpoint to this display of violence and horror in the person of Jawad Bendaoud who, happy to be on TV, repeated over and over: 'I was asked to help out, so I helped out.' This sketch went viral and earned the obliging slumlord the nickname Century 21. He was tried and acquitted in the first instance, then sentenced to four years in prison on appeal.

The building at 8 Rue du Corbillon was already unsanitary, and reputed to be a den of prostitutes and drug dealers. When it was destroyed the tenants were evacuated, given camp beds in a gym for several months, and never really rehoused after that. They lost everything, with no compensation. Often less of a big deal is made about the victims on the café terraces than those who were at the Bataclan. And less is made of the spectators at the Stade de France than about those on the terraces. But as the victims at the Rue du Corbillon weren't even victims of terrorism but of the anti-terrorist police, their claim to be included among the plaintiffs was not admissible in court. They were the poorest beforehand, they were the poorest after: the lumpenproletariat among the victims. Some of them summoned their courage and came to V13. In poor French, sobbing and sniffling, they did their best to make it clear that they had been harmed and were still harmed, even though they had escaped with their lives – a fact they were reminded of almost as a reproach. A Serbian woman came to the stand with her three-year-old daughter who ran around screaming the whole time, annoying the presiding judge in the process. If it had been the little daughter of a young blonde woman from the Bataclan, everyone would have been moved. It's a clear case of class justice; still, it's better not to venture too far down the slippery slope of double standards if you don't want to ask yourself the question someone like Vergès would ask: We make of our 131 dead a world event that we still commemorate seven years on. We hold a trial of historic proportions, shoot films, write books like this one. But 131 Syrians or Iraqis killed by American bombs (or by Bashar or Putin for that matter)? Nobody cares, it's a Reuters dispatch and that's that.

Chakib Akrouh's body was recovered in six pieces, which were cleaned and buried in the Islamic section of the Cemetery of Evere in Brussels.

A few days after 18 November, Sonia was declared dead. Her death certificate was registered. She no longer exists. Yet she came to the hearing. Like a shadow puppet. Her voice distorted, she recounted part of what you've just read, and explained what happened to her after that. 'What you did was very courageous,' the prosecutor François Molins told her solemnly, after which she and her family were led out by a service called the

SIAT (Inter-ministerial Service for Technical Assistance), which for the past seven years has allowed her and her family to live in total secrecy. They've changed their identities, their place of residence, their civil status – like Salman Rushdie and Roberto Saviano. Her children have grown up in this twilight zone, under the radar, always moving, always fearing they'll be asked for a document they don't have, always at the mercy of a quizzical look. If anyone recognises them it could mark the beginning of the end. The system that protects them is modelled on programmes set up in Italy for the *pentiti*, or repentant members of the Camorra and Red Brigades. The word 'repentant' is little suited to the case of a woman who saved dozens of lives by bidding farewell to a normal life for herself and her family. Sonia has not repented – why should she? – but above all she does not regret her decision, she tells us. Even knowing the labyrinth she'd be walking into, she would do it all over again. If Sonia isn't a heroine, I don't know who is.

Salah Abdeslam's final version

On the slide

Whether it was planned with his lawyers or not, Salah Abdeslam's defence strategy consists of putting off until as late as possible, even to the point of absurdity, the moment when he realised that everything he'd been doing since the summer of 2015 had in fact played a role in preparing the attacks. The five trips to Hungary or Germany to 'go and look for people'? Humanitarian repatriation. Renting cars and flats? To help Muslims in need – just as others help Ukrainian refugees today. Buying fireworks equipment? To set off fireworks, what else? And the dinner with his fiancée on 10 November, during which he started crying because he was going to leave and would never see her again? He was about to leave for al-Sham. There is not a shred of evidence for such a plan, no preparations of any kind, no ticket to Turkey: nothing. In short, Salah Abdeslam saw nothing, heard nothing and suspected nothing until 11 November, when his brother Brahim takes him to Charleroi to meet with Abdelhamid Abaaoud, who's waiting for him in his hideout. He hasn't seen Abaaoud for almost two years, he had no idea that he was back in Belgium. And

now Abaaoud tells him straight out that he's been chosen
to blow himself up in Paris in two days. In two days!
Mohamed Abrini says he was recruited in the same way
in September: two months beforehand is more plausible
than two days. Just for the sake of it, let's assume that
this is not an out-and-out lie. The only possible explanation for this incredibly late date would be that Abdeslam
was recruited at the last minute to replace Abrini, who'd
pulled out. This is what Abrini himself says, the only
problem being that he's incapable of saying exactly when
that was. Not two days before the attacks take place, not
before the death convoy sets off, maybe not before they
arrive in Bobigny, and maybe, quite simply, not at all.
Abrini and Abdeslam have spent the entire trial next to
each other in the box. The whole time they've been talking and laughing. Then as the final interrogations
approached their interaction became more strained, and
Judge Périès had to separate them. And now they're presenting conflicting accounts as ultimate truths. 'You
shouldn't believe everything Abrini says,' Abdeslam says
condescendingly, 'although sometimes he does tell the
truth.' Above all one gets the feeling lately that they're
both trying to hog the limelight at the trial. Let's backtrack. On the afternoon of 11 November, Salah
Abdeslam sees Abaaoud. All through the night of the
11th, he reflects. He understands that he won't be able to
do what's being asked of him. He doesn't have the fire in
his belly, killing people is not for him – which is also
what Abrini said to himself, or so he says. But he's already

on the slide. The next afternoon the death convoy sets off for Paris. He's driving the Clio. Brahim is writing text messages in the back. No nasheeds in this version. Abrini is silent. To believe them, two of the three future suicide bombers are determined not to go through with it – only they're keeping that to themselves for the moment. No doubt they're scared to open up to Brahim – let alone to Abaaoud. Neither account mentions the obvious fact that when you're taking part in an Islamic State attack, announcing the day before that you have a bad feeling about the whole thing cannot go down well. You've got to expect a different reaction from 'Man, are you a pain in the arse, brother, we were *counting on* you . . .' Does Abrini suspect what's going on in Abdeslam's head? Does Abdeslam suspect what's going on in Abrini's head? They arrive in Bobigny. Brahim gives Salah his explosive belt but they don't talk about what will happen the next day. They eat in silence, knowing that, all going to plan, in twenty-four hours they'll all be dead – except Abrini, who leaves without saying goodbye, and without us knowing how the others took it. He doesn't tell us, and Abdeslam, who could, doesn't either.

The café on the corner

And then it's the 13th. Salah Abdeslam, apparently, has still not voiced his reservations. In the early afternoon, he and Brahim leave in a taxi to scout the locations. Or more exactly, Brahim shows his younger brother his targets. The mission: first he has to drop off the three human bombs at the Stade de France. Then he must go and blow himself up in a café in the 18th arrondissement. This café is a novelty, and a particularly unlikely one. All of the other members of the commando were recruited months beforehand and would be acting in groups of three. Who could believe that the least experienced of them all, the one who'd been recruited from the sidelines two days earlier, would be sent to act alone? The only thing we learn about this mysterious café which emerged like a rabbit from a hat is that it was on a street corner. Not much more is known about what the two brothers said to each other during this last trip together. When they get back to Bobigny it's already time to leave, they're even a little late. Salah gets into the Clio with the two Iraqis, who don't speak a word of French, and Bilal Hadfi, who's sweating profusely because he's no longer so sure he wants to die at twenty. Unfortunately when they were scouting they misjudged the time it would take to get to the Stade de France, or their scouting trip lasted too long, in any case they arrive late and the doors of the stadium are closed. Instead of the planned massacre there will be only one death, in addition to the three suicide bombers in their Bayern Munich jerseys. But Abdeslam knows nothing about this. He drops the three of them off and leaves, without waiting for the sound of the explosions. He drives to the café on the corner in the

18th arrondissement. He parks the car. Goes to the counter. Orders a drink. It's the first time he's been alone since they left Charleroi the day before. He looks around him. Young people, very young, having fun. Some are dancing. With a nice shirt and some scent behind his ears, he could be one of them. It's clear, he can't go through with it. He's not cut out for it. In the heat of the moment, swept along by the others, maybe, but not here. Brahim, who's going to blow himself up or has just blown himself up at Le Comptoir Voltaire, didn't take the time to stop and look at the people. Once you've stopped, once you've looked at the people, you can forget it. He gets back into the Clio, which breaks down. He abandons it. He goes into a phone shop and buys a cheap phone into which he slips a blank SIM card, bought a few weeks earlier under the name of Pierre Loti – a nineteenth-century French writer whose role is as mysterious here as that of Sacha Guitry in the computer picked up on the Rue Max Roos. He calls his friend Mohammed Amri and says he's had a 'bad crash'.

The bad crash

Just what is this bad crash? A breakdown, an accident, a brawl after a prang with another car? He didn't say, and Amri didn't think to ask. Amri says he can't help him out, he's working. Abdeslam insists, he's in deep shit. Okay, says Amri, we'll see what we can do, I'll call Attou.

With the little money he has left, Abdeslam takes a taxi
to the suburbs south of Paris. The massacre is all over
the news. He never imagined how big a thing it would
be. The driver, a North African, laments: 'They'll make
us Muslims pay for this!' Abdeslam: 'That only height-
ens my distress.' (In a general way he's very alive to his
own distress.) In Montrouge he deactivates the suicide
belt as best he can, perhaps at the risk of his life, and
discards it in a bin. Not far from there in Châtillon he
eats a burger in a Quick fast-food restaurant, then takes
refuge in the Vauban housing estate – why Châtillon?
why the Vauban estate? – where he joins a group of
young people smoking in a stairwell. They talk about the
attacks, look at images of the terraces and the Bataclan
on a phone. Nothing is known about the taxi driver, but
the young people have been located. They remember
him and say he was nice and even smiled, although he
seemed nervous. He tells them about his fiancée, says he
loves her and is afraid he could lose her. Every so often
he disappears in the stairwell to make a phone call. We
know that he's calling Amri and Attou. At one point he
falls asleep on the steps, leaning against the wall, his
head in his parka. At 5.30 a.m., Amri and Attou arrive.
They describe him as haggard and in a state of shock.
He describes them as being in a state of shock as well,
because they've finally understood what's really going
on and what the bad crash is. They take the Boulevard
Périphérique to the north of Paris, and from there they
drive straight to Brussels. Abdeslam would rather use

the secondary roads, but they're blocked. He'd also like to stop at a hotel, but the other two don't want to. One imagines them in Amri's Golf: a daydream, or more like a feverish nightmare. They arrive in Molenbeek. Ali Oulkadi takes over from Amri and Attou – I'll tell that part of the story in the next section. Abdeslam joins the other members of the group in their hideout, the el-Bakraoui brothers, Najim Laachraoui, plus the eternal companion Abrini who opens the door for him. It's a difficult moment: he has to explain to the brothers that his belt didn't work. Disbelief, anger. Tempers flare, but he sticks to this version which he now repeats is a lie – the truth being that if he didn't blow himself up it wasn't because of a technical failure or cowardice but 'out of a sense of humanity'. From then on, he says, 'I don't ask any more questions. I have a place to stay, I'm there, I wait. I'd like to go to al-Sham but my face is everywhere, impossible to go out.' He goes from hideout to hideout until he's captured on 18 March, four days before the attacks on the Brussels metro and airport in which it's not known if he was to take part, but that's a matter for the upcoming Belgian trial and does not concern us here.

Solace

After stringing us along these past few days like a capricious starlet ('Sometimes I talk, sometimes I don't, depending on how you treat me and whether I like your

questions'), he delivers up his truth, the definitive version, the version for history, the way they say that V13 is
a trial for history, and this version is a tissue of incoher-
ences and unlikelihoods. It's spread out over three days
of questioning, and concludes with a sort of peroration
in dialogue form with his lawyer, Olivia Ronen, who is
excellent, no question about it, except that, also no question about it, I don't like how she calls him Salah in court.
In this final stretch and with her help, he manages to
move us. To hit the right note. He speaks of his mother,
sniffs back a convincing sob. He asks for forgiveness
from the three poor guys he got into shit, Amri, Attou,
Oulkadi, and from the victims – in whose ranks he clearly
also counts himself. He also says something strange,
something I see as both sincere and obscene. 'I don't
know if the victims bear any resentment towards me
(*resentment*!) but I say to them: don't let your resentment
choke you. There is a lot of darkness in this story, but
there is also a gleam of light . . . It may be insensitive to
say this in front of the victims, but that's how I felt on
hearing some of their testimonies. They've come out of
this ordeal stronger, they've become better, with qualities
you don't find at the supermarket . . .' I'm not going to
contradict him, I thought the same thing. Nevertheless
I'm not sure it's of any solace to the victims for him to
congratulate them on their fortitude. Flipping through
my notebooks from the beginning of the trial on this
Easter weekend, I come across another end to a testimony: 'When I got out of hospital I thought I was going

to enjoy life two hundred per cent. In fact I'm at best half of what I was before. There must be people for whom it's true that "what doesn't kill you makes you stronger", as they say. For me it's not. I'm still fighting, but in fact I've been given a life sentence.'

The exfiltrators

An easy number to remember

Is 0032486977742 an easy number to remember? This question was argued back and forth during the final questioning of Mohammed Amri. Abdeslam didn't take his phone with him when he went to blow himself up on the evening of the 13th: you don't need your phone to do that. When he decided not to go through with it and started looking for a way home he went to a shop and bought one, which of course did not have his contacts in it. So if he was able to call Amri it's because he knows his number by heart. Why does he know Amri's number by heart? Since mobile phones came in we've all known very few numbers by heart, often none at all. Because they were very close, says the prosecution – which is not good for Amri. Because the number is easy to remember, say Amri and his lawyers Negar Haeri and Xavier Nogueras. It's subjective, they maintain. 'In any case,' says Amri, 'I'd have preferred he didn't.' But unfortunately he does, and at 10.30 p.m. Amri receives the famous call from Abdeslam where he's working at the SAMU social in Molenbeek – a transit centre for asylum seekers – telling him that he's in France, that he's had 'a bad crash', and that he needs help. Abdeslam cries on the phone, just as he cried three days earlier when he told his fiancée he was leaving. He doesn't say exactly what kind of 'bad crash' he's had or where he is – in France, that's all – and when Amri learns a little later in the evening that there's been a terrible series of attacks in Paris, he doesn't make the connection. The prosecution doubts this, and argues that he knowingly went to rescue an Islamic State fighter. The defence paints him as a good-natured if naive guy who wouldn't let a friend down in a jam. A real friend, as everyone knows, is one you can call at 4 a.m. because you've done something stupid, and who turns up with the rug to hide the corpse with in the boot of his car. Amri is that kind of friend. He can't come right away, but thinks their friend Hamza Attou, a puny drug dealer who runs his business out of Les Béguines, might be able to. Attou has neither a car nor a driving licence; the licence is a minor point, but they definitely need a car. Abdeslam calls every five minutes, insists, cries. In the end Amri and Attou decide to go together. They could be a couple of comic-strip characters: the big, strong, kind and a bit slow Amri, and the little, fidgety, clever Attou, except that after smoking ten spliffs a day practically since he was a kid, Attou is even less on the ball than Amri. They leave in Amri's Golf at around one in the morning with the music playing, good and stoned as always. It's a normal trip, they're pretty laid-back and don't know they're on a highway to hell. The cashier at the petrol station where they stop to tank up tells Attou that some nasty stuff has happened in Paris. But Attou's not interested in the news, he doesn't have a smartphone, just two crappy dealer's phones costing 20 and 30 euros – pictures of which his lawyers will project onto the screen at the hearing to show how under-equipped and ill-informed he was. In short, when he's told about the attacks he doesn't catch on, and neither does Amri. At no point during the trip do they talk about it, and in fact, they both swear, they didn't even know they were going to Paris. Abdeslam gave them an address: 1 Allée Vauban in Châtillon, and they put it in the GPS without knowing that Châtillon is a suburb of Paris. It could have been in the highlands of central France, same diff.

In shock

5.30 a.m. – they find Abdeslam at the foot of a council estate in the middle of nowhere. He's not doing well at all, sweating heavily and breathing hard, and immediately says that he lied to them, that the big crash was that: these huge attacks. His brother Brahim was supposed to blow himself up, he doesn't know if he did or not, he was also supposed to blow himself up, he's the tenth member of the commando, they've got to hotfoot it back to Brussels. However stoned the two might have been, they high-dive into the state of feverish panic they both so convincingly describe. The prosecution and plaintiffs' lawyers will bombard them with rational questions, ignoring the obvious fact that they were not at all in a rational state of mind. Yes, if they'd been responsible citizens, they'd have said you get the hell out of this car, we came here to help a friend who did something stupid, not to protect a terrorist. Or escaped while he was in the toilet at the petrol station. Or called the police. If they'd known the penal difference between helping a criminal (not too serious) and helping a criminal linked to a terrorist act (you risk twenty years), they'd have thought twice about what they were doing. Unfortunately they weren't in a position to think twice about what they were doing. Amri keeps saying that he was 'in shock'. The term quickly becomes repetitive, you get the feeling his lawyers prompted him, nevertheless I think it describes his state exactly. The journey there was foggy but cool, the return trip a feverish nightmare. Abdeslam dozes in the back, his hood down. Amri relates that at one point he said to him, 'It's not right, what you did,' to which Abdeslam answered, 'Shut the fuck up, you know fuck all about religion.'

'This is going a bit far'

One very short scene, however, nuances the image of this journey as a feverish nightmare carried out in a state of shock by three tetanised men. Driving back on the motorway in the early hours of Saturday 14 November, they passed no less than three police checkpoints. At the first the officer took a look at their ID and waved them through – Abdeslam wasn't yet public enemy number one. At the second it was clear to the gendarmes that the car smelled like a hash pipe on wheels, but they had other things to worry about that night, so keep moving. That made Salah laugh, Amri remembers, and cheered him up a bit. Fooling the cops: that's a good one. No doubt that explains the relaxed atmosphere at the third checkpoint. There, at a motorway toll, a Belgian radio journalist asking drivers how they felt about all the road-blocks and mayhem held out her microphone to the three. It sounds crazy, but there really is an interview with Abdeslam, Amri and Attou in their car, taken around 7 a.m. on 14 November. We listened to it at the hearing, it lasts twenty seconds max, and the truth is that they don't seem to be in a state of shock at all. Rather they come across as three chatty little stoners who're slightly amused by the whole thing: 'Frankly, this is going a bit far.' 'Yeah, it's going too far . . .' 'But we heard what happened. So it's normal, I guess . . .' Okay, next.

Amri eats fried eggs

When they arrive in Brussels, Mohammed Amri has one obsession, and that's to go home, put his head under the pillow and tell himself that it was all a bad dream.

Abdeslam needs a change of clothes, a haircut, and one last driver to take him to the hideout in the Schaerbeek district to meet up with the others – rightly fearing how they might treat him when he gets there. For this stage of the journey Attou calls his buddy Ali Oulkadi, who comes over without a second thought, assuming it's for a drug deal – the basis of their relationship and, in general, of all of their interactions. No sooner does Oulkadi arrive than Amri splits for the metro, leaving Attou the keys to his beloved Golf. Judge Périès will ask him whether in his mind he'd accomplished his mission, and the question puzzles him: mission, what mission? It's like 'exfiltration' – a word he didn't even know. When he gets home around noon, his wife doesn't ask him where he's been or what he did all night. He says he helped out a friend, friends are sacred, she lets it rest. She makes him fried eggs. He eats them in silence. He tries to sleep, but can't. He knows he's in big, big trouble, so he's almost relieved when the police come to pick him up at 3.30 that afternoon. His wife, Kim Timmermans, is a midwife. When she testified at the trial, she impressed with her cocky good humour, her robust health and her unwavering loyalty. One feels she deserves a medal: Mohammed Amri is none too bright, you could say he's a loser, and he's been in prison for six years for getting caught up in a huge case of terrorism. Others would have left him, not Kim Timmermans. She hasn't abandoned him, hasn't rebuilt her life with anyone else, she's been going to visit him for six years and will be there when he gets out, if he gets out. Amri's lawyers present this blonde, blue-eyed, ruddy-cheeked Flemish woman not only as the chance of a lifetime for her husband, but also as the living proof, if any were needed, that he was not radicalised. Without denying her robust moral qualities, the prosecution nevertheless points out that on her Facebook page Kim refers to herself as a 'servant of Allah'. All of this is complicated.

The last link in the chain

Ali Oulkadi didn't know Salah Abdeslam very well. He was a friend and underling of Brahim. The last memory he has of Brahim dates from 11 November: a card game at Les Béguines. They had a falling-out, really nothing at all, but Brahim got all worked up, and in retrospect it struck Oulkadi as odd that he could get angry over a game of cards when two days later . . . There was nothing left to smoke, they called Attou who didn't answer, so Oulkadi decided to go home, saying okay, see you tomorrow. That was the last time he saw Brahim. As they saw each other almost every day he was surprised when he didn't hear from him, and at noon on Saturday the 14th, between 12.03 and 12.18, as Amri's Golf was approaching Brussels, he tried to call him seven times. He says he didn't make the connection between Brahim's silence and the attacks. The first images he saw of them were on the TV that morning, without sound, and he thought it was a robbery, something like that. When someone points out that there's no reason for the Belgian TV to report non-stop on a robbery in Paris he agrees, but there you go, that's what he thought. In any event Attou calls him at around 1 p.m. and he goes to see him in a café, where he's together with Amri, who takes off right away, and Salah Abdeslam, who's very nervous and keeps repeating that he's in big shit because everything's in his name, the cars, the flats, and that he's been 'tricked'. 'If I'd known he was involved in the attacks I wouldn't have reacted the same way,' Oulkadi says. 'At no time did I think that I was helping a terrorist. When you say terrorist I think of bin Laden. For me Salah wasn't a terrorist but a little guy from the neighbourhood, always nice, always smiling, so I assumed that he was in trouble. That he'd been tricked, as he said.' After that Attou leaves as well, and Abdeslam asks Oulkadi to drive him to a hideout in Anderlecht. Then he says no, Schaerbeek, drive me to Schaerbeek, and guides him. When they get there he rubs the glove compartment and door handle with a tissue before getting out. They smoke a cigarette on the pavement then say goodbye. Not sure what tone to strike, Oulkadi says: 'Well, see you then,' and Abdeslam replies that they'll never see each other again – which isn't true, they've been seeing each other every day for nearly eight months. Because he's not as close to the fugitive as the other two, Ali Oulkadi is only arrested a week later. He retains a vague memory of this week – you could see that you were in a bind, people around him said – and the persistent regret that he didn't go down to the police station and denounce himself as he'd constantly thought of doing, only to put it off again and again. For several days after the 13th, and although the names of the dead terrorists were officially known, he continued to send Brahim distressed text messages: *Are you okay? Where are you?*

The mascot

At the end of his last interrogation, Ali Oulkadi turned to Abdeslam: 'I'm so angry with you, Salah,' he said. 'You have no idea how angry I am. My life is broken, my family's a wreck, my father's lost half his weight, I'm obliged to tell my daughter that I've got a job in France and don't dare admit what I'm really doing here, all because of you and your brother. I didn't ask you for a thing, I've got nothing to do with all this. I'm not comparing myself with the victims, I'm just saying that I don't deserve this. And I thank everyone who speaks to me here, everyone for whom I'm not just one of the defendants in the 13 November trial, but Ali.' Oulkadi's obvious sincerity moves everyone. When the hearing gets out many of us surround him on the steps of the Palais de Justice and tell him that he spoke well, that we're confident that things will work out for him. A lot of the plaintiffs come up as well, it's said that a small group of them took him to visit the Bataclan. He became a kind of mascot of the trial, and I'm sure that if he were given a prison sentence the verdict would be greeted with dismay. When it was Abdeslam's turn the next day, he apologised to Amri, Attou and Oulkadi. And as much as his apology to the victims came across as stiff, when he apologised to the buddies from Molenbeek whose lives he shattered, I believed every word.

The Court

Let's talk money

Bread and butter

The victims have testified, the accused have been questioned, the facts have been reconstructed. V13 is entering its final phase. Pleadings on behalf of the plaintiffs, final words of the prosecution, pleadings by the defence, verdict. We'd hoped to be finished by mid-June, but the defendant Farid Kharkhach has Covid so things have been delayed by another week. Kharkhach is accused of forging IDs, so the joke is that he forged his test result. This delay worries everyone who's been planning to go away in July. The only advantage is that it leaves me with a vacant column and the space to address that taboo subject: money.

The price of tears

The plaintiffs come to the trial to have their sufferings heard and to obtain moral support, but not for financial reparations. Such compensation is dealt with elsewhere, in a different court that interests no one. No one, that is, except Mathieu Delahousse, my colleague from *L'Obs* at

V13. Every second Thursday morning for two years he's gone to the small white room on the sixth floor of the Judicial Court of Paris, which handles compensation for victims of terrorism. He's never run into another journalist there, and what he's brought back is a very lively, very human book*, whose title, which translates as 'the price of our tears', poses a dizzying question: how to set a price tag on sorrow? Harmed by a group of fanatics against whom your country failed to protect you, you have lost – the list varies from case to case and is unfortunately cumulative – a leg, your wife, your son, your best friend, your mobility, your psychological equilibrium, your ability to work, your income, your sleep, your confidence in life . . . All of this is irreparable, and yet your country must make reparations. It has undertaken to do so. It's to this end that the Guarantee Fund for Victims of Terrorist Acts and Other Offences was created in 1986. You may not know it, but everyone in France contributes to this fund, which is financed by a flat tax of 5 euros and 90 cents per year on all insurance contracts signed in the country. That's a lot of money to distribute. For severe physical damage it's done according to a scale called the Dintilhac nomenclature. For psychological trauma, which is more difficult to quantify, the basic rate is 30,000 euros, but that's not the end of it. You get 30,000 if you have nightmares. But if these

* Mathieu Delahousse, *Le Prix de nos larmes*, Éditions de l'Observatoire, 2022.

nightmares are disabling, if they prevent you from sleeping or make you lose your job, you can request more – and more often than not you get it. What the court deals with is the grey area over which the victims' lawyers and the fund's lawyers fight tooth and nail. Lawyers specialising in personal injury compensation take between eight and twelve per cent of the compensation they obtain, and are much less flamboyant, Mathieu tells us, than their colleagues in the criminal courts. Opposite them, the fund's lawyer, who throughout the book is a woman, has the thankless role of continually finding that the victims' demands are excessive, and that their damages are exaggerated or not sufficiently well established. You wouldn't have to push her very hard to make her say, like the far-right politician Jean-Marie Le Pen, that it's worse to lose your sister than your cousin, and worse to lose your cousin than your neighbour. But in fact this is one of the recurring questions that arise at the fund: can compensation go beyond bonds of kinship and marriage? Can you compensate bereaved friends? Can you reimburse psychotherapy and physiotherapy sessions – but not thalassotherapy? Can you pay the 800,000 euros demanded by a survivor because, without having lost his very lucrative job, he refused another, even more lucrative one due to post-traumatic stress? Can you assess the 'imminent death damage' suffered by someone killed at the Bataclan – the degree to which he or she suffered before dying – and calculate whether for this reason his or her spouse should receive greater compensation? . . .

Deeply empathetic, Mathieu Delahousse's book navigates between grief, anger, absurdity and a feeling of injustice . . . Nevertheless when I write the words 'feeling of injustice', rather than 'injustice' tout court, I'm walking on eggshells. I think of the many, many injured and bereaved people I meet at the trial, almost all of whom complain of the fund's cheapness and inhumanity. I understand them, I know that subjectively they're right; however, it should be remembered that no country has a fund for terror victims as protective as that of France – or with as large a budget. And that also goes for legal aid, a subject I'll turn to now.

The price of words

Legal aid is the system that allows everyone to have a lawyer paid for by the state if they can't afford one themselves. In terrorism cases it applies regardless of income. Everyone is entitled to it, defendants and plaintiffs alike. Knowing that in V13 there are fourteen defendants and – at the time I'm writing – around 2,400 plaintiffs, that makes for a lot of lawyers and a lot of money for those lawyers, all of whom are paid at the same rate: 272 euros before taxes per day and per case. That being said, there's a huge difference between the plaintiffs' lawyers and the lawyers for the defence. The plaintiffs' lawyers can have as many clients as they want. Some have only one, some have three, some have fifty, some firms are said to have over a hundred. Most of these firms, I'm sure, give their clients a great deal of individual attention. Nevertheless their knowledge of the case and the amount of work it represents are more or less constant whether they have one or one hundred. On the other side of the courtroom the situation is radically different: the defence lawyers can only have one client and, given the enormity of the case and the difficulty of mastering it, there are generally two or even three lawyers for every defendant. Unlike the plaintiffs' lawyers they're obliged to be present at all times, and their law office must dedicate itself entirely to the trial. Consequently various measures have been taken to correct this imbalance somewhat. For the plaintiffs' lawyers a sliding scale has been put in place: the more clients they have, the less they get per client. And after heated discussions it was agreed that around ten per cent of what the plaintiffs' lawyers are due should be paid to the defence lawyers so they don't work at a loss. There are no official figures on this highly contentious issue so it's only a ballpark figure, nevertheless it can be said that a defence lawyer will receive roughly 50,000 euros over the duration of the trial, while some of the plaintiffs' lawyers will rake in over a million and a half. Please note: I am not speaking ill of the plaintiffs' lawyers, some of whom are simply excellent. But I am speaking well of the defence lawyers. In some cases they earn a tenth of what they would earn on the other side, while their tasks are ten times weightier. Most of them are young, at the start of their careers, it's said this will make them known to a wider audience, which is true. But one can also say that they do it for the beauty of the gesture and the love of justice, which comes down to wanting to defend that which is the most difficult to defend. Defending victims is noble, and essential, but the cause is won in advance. Defending alleged terrorists is something else altogether. You have to want to do it, you have to like a fight. What's more, there will always be people who'll put you in the same boat as your clients: birds of a feather flock together. One thing I find beautiful about V13 is that such prejudices are rare. Most of the victims I talk to have a high regard for the lawyers of the accused. They think it's important that they should be good. I remember Nadia, who concluded her testimony by turning to them. 'Now, defence lawyers, do your job. Do it well. I mean it.'

You can't kill rock'n'roll

'It's going to be tough'

Over the past month it's become a ritual: every time we run into lawyers for the plaintiffs at the coffee machine during the breaks, we ask as if they were seriously ill: 'How are you getting on? Are you going to make it?' They shrug and answer: 'No choice, right?' Sigh. '. . . but it's going to be tough.' What's going to be tough? The closing speeches. The plaintiffs' lawyers represent the victims. But in this trial they don't really have to fight for them to prove that they've suffered and deserve reparations – as you would, say, when you plead against a large corporation charged with institutional moral harassment. You can plead against a company, sure, but who's going to plead against the Islamic State? Throughout the trial the role of the plaintiffs' lawyers has been to support their clients, accompany them, prepare them to testify and if necessary hold out a box of tissues, a job most of them did with apposite delicacy. But now? One wants to say: they must give a voice to the victims' suffering. The problem is that the victims have already given a voice to their suffering. They did it over a period of five weeks, with an extraordinary collective eloquence, and moved everyone very deeply. What can their lawyers add that's not at best superfluous, at worst obscene? That's the first pitfall. The second, given that they can't give a voice to the victims' suffering, is to try to reiterate the arguments of the prosecution. Because that's not their role. Certainly, it could be if the three public prosecutors were in any way deficient, but they're all brilliant and know the case like no one else: it would serve no purpose to tread on their ground. So then what? How to navigate between these two hazards? Especially as these final statements will last for nine days and some 150 of the 350 counsel for the plaintiffs intend to have their say. Lawyers are a guild rich in flamboyant personalities and strong egos, so it comes as no surprise that, between plenary sessions and hallway haggling, they've been at loggerheads for a month now over just how this pleading will go. Some announced at the start that they'd only represent their clients and themselves. Others, among them most of those present, have set up a sort of collective pleading system to progress coherently from one topic to the next, with each lawyer dealing with a different subject. Here are some, chosen at random: 'Does evil unite us?', 'Failure and vulnerability', 'The freedom to hate and not to hate', 'The taste for pleasure', 'Finding the words', 'Love' ... And why not? In any case nobody is going to listen to everybody, at least not me. We've been rubbing shoulders with these lawyers practically every day now for eight months. With time we've got to know them well. We know which ones we like, and which ones make us yawn even before they open their mouths. We have the schedule, and like at the French Open tennis tournament, we'll select the ones we want to see. We start putting crosses in front of their names.

The guard of honour

The guy's wearing a black suit, a black shirt and a red tie. He's got a big red moustache, a low-slung ponytail, the blotchy complexion of a seasoned beer drinker, and a beautiful, deep, self-confident voice which he modulates like a musician playing an instrument. He could be a televangelist, he's a singer. He's Jesse Hughes, frontman of the Eagles of Death Metal, the rock band that played at the Bataclan on 13 November 2015. His account is standard, punctuated with some very American-sounding clichés – 'my love affair with Paris', 'you can't kill rock'n'roll . . .' – still, all things considered he comes across as modest and likeable. The surprising moment comes when, having finished his testimony, he turns and heads for the exit. In front of him the aisle is lined on either side with white wooden benches – I'd never noticed how much the V13 courtroom resembles a modern church: clear and bright despite the absence of windows. Along this aisle which is some forty metres long, a guard of honour composed entirely of survivors of the Bataclan attack has formed. And not just any survivors: the band's fans, the rockers, the real ones, with their tattooed biceps, leather jackets, and rings in their ears. If it had been allowed, they'd be clasping their pints of beer. Jesse Hughes walks over and stops at the first one. They look at each other, smile. Jesse takes him in his arms. He hugs him for a moment, a long moment. When they part, they both have tears in their eyes. He moves on to the next, and then the next. I don't know how many of them there are, thirty or forty, each one gets his or her hug, it comes naturally, without a show, Napoleon pulling his soldiers' ears, the tears welling up, the warmth, the huge wave of friendship among survivors, it's an incredibly moving moment, and I no longer think it's a cliché at all to say you can't kill rock'n'roll.

The intruder

On 13 November 2016, the Eagles of Death Metal returned to Paris for a concert commemorating the first anniversary of the attacks. It was followed, backstage, by the same kind of procession, the same succession of hugs and tears. A photo shows, dressed in a rocker's outfit and in the arms of Jesse Hughes, the same Flo whose story I told at the beginning of the trial – how far away that now seems . . . She claimed to be a Bataclan survivor. She'd become the webmaster and then a member of the managing board of the association Life for Paris. Her empathy, her resilience, her zeal to unmask the imposters who'd wormed their way into the circle of victims were exemplary. It was all fake – except for her misery, and her joy at that moment.

Two broken ribs

Jesse Hughes's appearance was the most eagerly awaited, indeed the only appearance awaited at all during this bizarre week devoted to the final testimonies before the lawyers' last statements. Right up until the end of the trial, victims who did not testify in the autumn have the right to change their minds and be heard. Some eighty have signed up to take the stand. This booster shot, although it's not at all a boon for the defence, is no doubt useful, and brings home to us once more the sheer horror that underlies this trial. This time around, however, we don't listen with the same fervour as in October. At one point I had a horrible thought: if you were to make a film about the trial, these are scenes you'd want to cut. Not because they're bad, but because they're redundant. We've seen it all, heard it all before, they add nothing. But in fact that's not true. Among other speakers I think of this young man who was twenty-one at the time, and who came out of the Bataclan unscathed. For three years he was totally disconnected. No memories. Only a malaise, the impression that people looked at him strangely. Dark but vague ideas. Nightmares without images. Indistinct silhouettes on the edge of his vision. A perpetual hangover that he cures with alcohol. The feeling that he's done something wrong, but what? It slips away. After three years he does EMDR therapy, a treatment now used for everything but which was invented for patients suffering from post-traumatic stress. Suddenly everything comes back. He knows what he did wrong. To reach the exit he pushed, crushed and trampled his way through the crowd. He became a survival machine that didn't give a rat's arse about anything else. He used the people he held the most dearly as human shields, just to stay alive. So he lives, yes, but he lives a damaged life. Others were heroes, he was not. Again and again he sees himself pushing, crushing, trampling. This film will run over and over in his head until the day he dies. He's ashamed. That's why he's here. To ask forgiveness from those he trampled underfoot. If one of them is here to hear him, at least that's something. He sobs. He leaves. I leave too: enough for today. The next day a lawyer friend tells me I missed something – that's a rule of thumb in court reporting: you always miss something when you decide to leave. Right after the young man racked with guilt, it was the turn of another Bataclan survivor. Much more relaxed, he began his testimony by saying that he'd just heard the young man speak before him, and wanted to tell him this: someone stepped on me and I had two broken ribs. *Just* two broken ribs. Maybe it was you who stepped on me, maybe it was someone else, we'll never know. But if it was you, you should know: two broken ribs is no big deal. I got over it, I'm alive, I'm happy, I don't blame you, you did what you could, we all did what we could, I hope you're still here to hear this. The young man was gone, but my lawyer friend ran out into the hall to look for him. She caught up with him outside on the steps of the Palais de Justice. If we were making a film, we'd stop at this image.

Anguish of imminent death

The last minute

You board the plane. You fasten your seat belt. In the middle of the aisle, the stewardess demonstrates what to do in case of an emergency. You listen to her absently. During the flight some people never think, others think only fleetingly, and others, the grand doomsayers, spend their entire time thinking about what statistically has very little chance of happening and yet does sometimes happen. It took one minute for the China Eastern Airlines Boeing 737 aircraft to stall and plunge 6,000 metres on 21 March 2022. Its 123 passengers had one minute to look death in the eye, with no way out, no doubt as to their fate. No one will know how each of them experienced that last minute. No one knows what goes on inside the head of someone who is about to die. About this experience which is so intimate, so incommunicable, the law nevertheless has something to say. It has a name which is not only psychological and philosophical but also legal, and which appeared in French law in 2005 following another air disaster: the 'anguish of imminent death'.

Doing law

For the past eight days, the plaintiffs' lawyers have been tacking back and forth between noble platitudes and quotations of famous authors, with Albert Camus in the lead. But some of them bring up weightier issues. Frédéric Bibal, a man with a compact build, closely cropped hair and round glasses, whose law firm deals with personal injury compensation, started with an observation: many victims found it a relief to come to the stand and give their depositions, precisely because they felt they were *depositing* something, letting it go. A suffering, a burden, something the court could take in. Many of them came out lightened, if only by a little. If the trial had only served this purpose, it would not have been in vain. But, says Bibal, that's not all. There's more to a deposition than paraphrasing or pathos – otherwise you might as well remain seated and go straight to the closing arguments. No, once taken in, the deposition must be moulded, shaped, fashioned into law. That's why we're here. And it's why Bibal laid out the notion of the anguish of imminent death, which the law defines as 'the feeling of terror experienced by the victim who, between the moment he or she suffered the attack or aggression and his or her death, was aware of the ineluctability of his or her demise'. This feeling of terror and ineluctability need not be the result of a violent death. One can die in one's own bed, prostrate from age, surrounded by one's loved ones, and still view one's approaching end with terror. But such terror is different, it's intimate and metaphysical. It unfolds between oneself and oneself, or between oneself and God – for those who use that term to refer to the deepest part of themselves. It does not concern the law. The law comes into play when there is violence, liability, damage and reparation. These are legal axioms: for all violence there is liability, all damage is subject to reparation – whether by the airline, the insurance company or the state. And if you're dead, it's your family who'll be compensated. This compensation will cover not only the grief and material damage caused by losing you, but also the suffering that *you*, the deceased, endured, and which you are no longer alive to describe. Here I hesitate as things get a bit technical; however, in the end technicalities are the only bulwark against 'anything goes' so here we go. Two chapters ago when I spoke about my colleague Mathieu Delahousse's book that deals with 'the price of our tears', I mentioned the 'Dintilhac nomenclature'. It lists the damages – physical, psychological and financial – suffered by the victims of attacks, in particular terrorist attacks, which give rise to a right to compensation. The anguish of imminent death is included here under the heading 'suffering endured', and is compensated within this overall budget framework. A decision of the French Court of Cassation dated 23 March 2022, however, counters that no, the anguish of imminent death is an autonomous damage, and gives rise to a right to autonomous compensation. In concrete terms, what that means is that if, in addition to your being killed, it can be proved that you died in anguish, your family will get more money. In penal terms it has another consequence, namely that the damage, in becoming autonomous, also gives rise to an autonomous reason for judgement on the part of the court. When this court delivers its judgement, which all going well it will do on 27 June, it will present what's known as a 'motivation sheet', listing the reasons for its verdict. What Bibal demands at the end of his remarks is that the anguish of imminent death of the victims of 13 November should figure autonomously in the court's reasons for judgement and sentencing. And, consequently, that those upon whom sentence will be passed will also be sentenced specifically for this. That is, for having participated not only in the death of 131 people, but also in the terror which most of them endured when faced with imminent death. On the face of it that doesn't change much, the sentences will be heavy enough as it is. But it's a way of taking in what has been said, and instead of scattering it to the four winds, of transforming it into law. And that is what a trial is, or should be: at the beginning suffering is deposited, at the end justice is rendered.

One hundred and thirty-one ways to die

The first question families ask is: did he suffer? Did she suffer? Who can answer? The forensic pathologists, the surviving witnesses. When they say that no, he or she died on the spot without grasping what was happening, that's a consolation. One may not have known that the anguish of imminent death was a legal concept, but it's a consolation not to be compensated for it. It's also a consolation to know that the last minutes before the tragedy were happy, carefree. That Lamia was mowed down at La Belle Équipe while having a romantic tête-à-tête with her boyfriend, and that they went from pure joy to nothingness together. At the Stade de France and on the terraces, the surprise effect was absolute. At the Bataclan the shooting lasted a good ten minutes: those who escaped the first bursts had plenty of time to be afraid. For five weeks in October and a further week in May, survivors told stories of instant deaths and prolonged agonies. I wrote down dozens of them, and I read them over now as we near the end of the trial. Here's what Maia, the young woman who was at the Carillon, said: 'At one point I feel death behind me. There's a guy right up close, pressed against my back. I hear him gasp and wheeze, I know these are his last moments. I know that I'm experiencing the last moments of his life. It's something very intimate, perhaps the most intimate thing you can share with someone. I'm the only witness to his death. I will never know his name.'

A quote

'She stayed by the door looking at me. And then – I don't know how to tell you exactly, but she shut her eyes, she began to shake her head, very slowly, and wring her hands, very slowly, and to whimper, or whisper. I couldn't understand what she was saying. But it broke my heart, I never felt so sorry for anyone, and I hugged her. I said, "Please, Bonnie! Oh, don't, darling, don't! If ever anyone was prepared to go to God, it was you, Bonnie." But I couldn't comfort her. She shook her head, and wrung her hands, and then I heard what she was saying. She was saying, "To be murdered. To be murdered. No. No. There's nothing worse. Nothing worse than that. Nothing." *

* Truman Capote, *In Cold Blood*, Random House, 1966.

The knights of penal law

Kill the adversary?

The scene takes place in the immense library, all leather and gold patina, of the Paris Bar Association. Young men and women in black robes and white bands stand in turn to plead on a given topic, one loosely related to the guest who presides over the session. Tonight: 'Should we kill the adversary?' – because the invited guest is me and I wrote a book called *The Adversary*. If I'd written *In Search of Lost Time*, I guess it could have been 'Should we waste our time?' Each speaker may choose to answer the question in the affirmative or the negative, the sport consisting in switching from one to the other, that is to argue for everything and its opposite. We're at a session of the Conférence du Stage, a months-long oratory contest in which some two hundred young lawyers have competed for the twelve top spots every year for the past two centuries. Designated by the winners of the previous year, the chosen twelve are called secretaries of the Conférence, and in the entire profession nothing is more prestigious. The arguments were funny, brilliant, the speakers taking the exercise perfectly seriously without taking themselves seriously at all. It made you want to join them at the brasserie Les Deux Palais where they show up late in the evening, overworked, laughing, feverish, with criminal files and crumpled robes sticking out of their oversized briefcases. I was thrilled with the invitation in any event, but I had an extra reason to be happy because the concluding speeches of the defence counsel at V13 start next week, and a good half of the lawyers for the defence are former secretaries of the Conférence. That's the case of Negar Haeri and Xavier Nogueras, who are defending Mohammed Amri and to whom I spoke about how they got where they are now.

Bow to the evidence?

Everyone at V13 calls Negar Haeri Negar, even those who don't know her personally, and I've never heard anyone say anything but good about her. She's a graceful, precise young woman with huge black eyes and black hair. She's of Iranian origin, fashionable and cultivated, with two brothers who are lawyers like her and who like her were secretaries of the Conférence. She wanted to be a pianist, she studied the piano for fifteen years and still plays – very well but not well enough in her view. So she does law the way she'd play a sonata: measure by measure, with great scrutiny, deciphering the rulings of the Court of Cassation the way she'd analyse a piece by Scriabin. Her subject at the Conférence in the year she became secretary: 'Should we bow to the evidence?' (She chooses the negative: even to the evidence she will not bow down.) For one year the secretaries must act as assigned counsel and defend the toughest cases free of charge, with duty days at the Palais de Justice. As soon as a crime is committed in Paris they're assigned to it, and every second case is sordid: it's a school of hard knocks of which they're proud. Negar served as secretary in 2015, their group photo was taken on 7 January – the day the satirical magazine *Charlie Hebdo* was attacked – and it's hard not to see that as a sign. One day while she was on duty at the courthouse, fifteen hooded gendarmes came in escorting a man who was also hooded: Mohammed Amri, who drove Salah Abdeslam from Paris back to Brussels on the morning of 14 November. After eight months of this trial we know him well, Amri: a big, clumsy guy who's a little slow and slurs his speech. Negar says she was touched by his inability to express himself, because as a child she learned to speak Farsi before she learned French, and she often still feels awkward and illegitimate in her adopted language. Considering what a brilliant orator she is that seems ludicrous; nevertheless I'm sure that from her point of view it's true, and with that in common the two forged a bond of trust over the sessions, with the result that Amri is one of the few defendants who hasn't changed lawyers in the past six years. That said, the case is monstrously huge and the firm has other business to attend to, so to keep the boat afloat Negar calls Xavier Nogueras.

Should we eat the fat?

Two years Negar's senior at the Conférence du Stage, Nogueras has a completely different profile. He too was given music lessons – piano, harpsichord, guitar, flute, trumpet – although less for the love of the art per se than to get him back on the straight and narrow. A native of Nice, half poser and half ruffian, he has a rather difficult family background which I take the liberty of telling because he makes no secret of it himself. His father was an examining magistrate. A seductive high roller, he died when Xavier was nine, leaving his family in difficulty but also with a trail of mystery: was it pulmonary embolism? Suicide? Twenty years later Xavier will learn the truth by chance from a forensic pathologist who describes an autopsy he performed on a judge who'd got hooked on cocaine while dealing with drug cases and died of an overdose. Weighed down by this double heritage – love of the law, love of risk – the son slacks off in his teens and dabbles in the theatre, until he goes with a buddy to a session of the Conférence du Stage. Bingo: this is the rostrum he's been looking for. As he says: 'I have all the narcissistic flaws to be a criminal lawyer.' His topic in the oratory contest: 'Should we eat the fat?' (He chooses the affirmative: yes, we should.) He serves as secretary in 2013, just after Mohamed Merah's attack on the Jewish school in Toulouse. Terrorism is becoming the daily bread of the knights of penal law who are the secretaries of the Conférence. The judges start sending away not only the newly radicalised on their way back from Syria, but also those who are arrested before they can leave although they've done nothing wrong, because they're liable to in the future. Such precautions may be understandable, but the law does not accept preventive justice and someone like Nogueras defends not only the 'terros', as they're called, but also the law. The job is frowned upon and not very lucrative: all the more reason to give himself up to it with no holds barred. The terros make up eighty per cent of his clientele, to the point that one day on the news a banner appears under his striking, bizarre face with white hair and different-coloured eyes, presenting him as 'Xavier Nogueras, lawyer for jihadist networks'. So all is as it should be.

To be the last to reach out a hand?

The day I'm arrested for a crime, they're the ones I'll call. She's a classical musician, he's a dandy and a punk at heart, their rigour and courtesy earned them the heartfelt respect of the court, the plaintiffs and the prosecution alike: the general consensus is that Amri is in good hands. The stakes are clear as far as he is concerned. Having exfiltrated Salah Abdeslam: criminal association. That'll get you put away for a good six years. He'll have served them come July; if the court contents itself with that he'll go free. But he's also accused of accompanying Abdeslam when he rented cars. That may seem more benign but it can be construed as criminal terrorist association: twenty years. His lawyers' whole strategy, which they've been practising since the beginning of the trial as if they were advancing pieces in a chess game, is aimed at dropping the T and reducing the charge to criminal association tout court. I'm not going to anticipate their final statements on 14 June. For now I'll just relate what Nogueras said to me over a glass of white wine at the brasserie Les Deux Palais when I put to him the eternal question: where do you draw the line? Are there any causes you'd refuse to defend? 'Just asking the question shows that you haven't understood what it is to be a lawyer,' he said. 'There's no cause that I defend, but there's no accused that I'll refuse. Vergès defended causes. He wasn't only defending Pol Pot or Carlos, but also what they did, what they stood for. He agreed with it. To take the crimes that are viewed with the most distaste, we obviously do not defend paedophilia or terrorism. But we are prepared to defend a paedophile or a terrorist. They *must* be defended, that's the law. Of course I sometimes find it difficult: it's easier to defend a robber I can go out with for a drink when he gets out than someone who gets his kicks out of watching beheading videos, but you've got to distinguish between the person and the act. That's what being a lawyer is all about: doing everything you can to ensure that the accused is judged according to the law and not according to sentiment. And, when everyone else has turned their backs, to be the last to reach out a hand.'

The torn curtain

Good work

As the end of the trial approaches one thinks back to the beginning, to the path we've taken. To what will have happened inside each one of us from the moment we entered this giant white wooden box on 8 September, to the verdict scheduled for 29 June. I remember the first day. The presiding judge took the floor to say that this trial, which everyone was right in saying was extraordinary, should take place in strict respect for the rule of law, and that only on this condition would it be exemplary. All in all that's how things have been, which is no small matter in itself. This is what the chief public prosecutor Camille Hennetier said to the court at the end of her closing remarks last Friday: 'Terror is the disappearance of the curtain which veils nothingness, and which normally allows us to live in peace. Terror is the impossibility of tranquillity. Your verdict will not repair the torn curtain. It will not heal the wounds, be they visible or invisible. It will not bring the dead back to life. But it can at least reassure the living that here law and justice have the last word.' From the beginning of V13 to the end I've been impressed by the quality of the prosecution. Three

magistrates from the national counter-terrorism prosecution service, a woman seconded by two men, all three
young, all three of whom were involved in the case from
day one and know it inside out. Always precise, never
showy, never a question out of place: they set the bar
very high. The prosecution's closing remarks spanned
three days – a judicial first – and curiosity was piqued.
Speaking in turn for roughly two hours at a time, Camille
Hennetier, Nicolas Braconnay and Nicolas Le Bris did
something extraordinary: they reviewed the whole trial
from the start, gathering up its strands and telling them
all over again. The narrative principle behind the trial was
a sort of chronological chaptering, which was inevitable
but frustrating: personality, radicalisation, Syria, the last
year, the last months, the last weeks, the last days . . .
From one chapter to the next, the threads became distended, frayed. They wove them back into place. That
involves narration, storytelling: as a man of the trade
whose job it is to tell stories, I admired the virtuosity with
which they did it: since you can't say everything, choosing
the most significant details with care. Placing the portraits of the accused in the right places, clarifying the role
each one played in the death machine, the precise charges
against him. Stressing that we will never know everything, but that they, those in the box, do. Explaining that
remaining silent is a right but so is lying, and that they
made as much use of the latter as of the former. The
only downside to this exemplary work of synthesis and
pedagogy: compared to what has already been laid out in

the OMA – the order of indictment summarising everything that was known about the defendants and their roles before the trial – how much more do we know now? What did the nine months of hearings add? In fact, not much: in terms of information, maybe ten, fifteen per cent. Everything regarding the victims and what we learned about humanity in listening to them was immense. But regarding those in the box? Like everyone else, I pondered about Salah Abdeslam's state of mind to the point of nausea. Did his suicide belt fail to go off? Was he afraid? Did he have a last-minute flash of humanity? Were his apologies sincere? But when all is said and done, what does it matter? What if anything is interesting about Salah Abdeslam's states of mind? A poor mystery: an abysmal void wrapped in lies, which one regrets with stunned amazement having spent so much time thinking about at all.

Intimate conviction

The sentencing demands are heavy and nuanced. For Salah Abdeslam, the only defendant considered to be a co-author of the attacks, life imprisonment with a whole life order: a real, 'incompressible' life sentence, which is practically never handed down. For the eternal companion Mohamed Abrini, as well as for Mohamed Bakkali, Osama Krayem and Sofien Ayari, the entire cell of highly placed Islamic State operatives, very heavy sentences with twenty to thirty years without remission – which is enormous but less uncommon. For the 'thwarted operatives' Adel Haddadi and Muhammad Usman, who should have participated in the attacks but couldn't because they were arrested in Vienna, the same. They must be punished as if they had, the prosecution insists. For Abdellah Chouaa, Hamza Attou and Ali Oulkadi, whom Camille Hennetier calls the 'small-timers', there may be a chance of leniency. Hennetier credits the three for respecting their bail conditions and coming to the trial obediently every day even though it was by no means easy – they live in Belgium, can no longer work, and have to get by in Paris with practically no money. Their lawyers hope they can get them off the hook, meaning they could go free. For a moment, now, I imagine that I'm a juror – or a judge since there's no jury in this trial. Before the court retires to deliberate, as it will in two weeks' time, I'm read Article 353 of the French Code of Criminal Procedure: 'The law requires each of the judges and jurors to question themselves in silence and recollection, and to seek, in the sincerity of their conscience, what impression the evidence brought against the accused, and the means of his defence, has made on their reason. The law only asks them this one question, which contains the full measure of their duties: Do you have an intimate conviction?' Today, yes, I do. It is that of Camille Hennetier, Nicolas Braconnay and Nicolas Le Bris. As they've presented it, the evidence brought against the accused has made a great impression on my reason. If I were a juror I would follow their recommendations. But the rule of French legal procedure is that the counsels for the defence have the last word. They will speak for two weeks. The thirty or so lawyers seated in front of the box are young and bright too. They'll be firing on all cylinders. What seemed obvious to me, irrefutable even, throughout the prosecution's closing remarks will then seem less obvious. Everything will be taken up once again and turned this way and that, each one of the prosecution's arguments will be, if not twisted, then minimised, recontextualised more or less in good faith to meet the needs of the speaker. Doubt – which as we know benefits the accused – will creep in. And that's a good thing. I don't know if this characteristic would make me a good judge or a bad one, but I'm easily convinced. I have no difficulty going along with other people's reasoning, which is both a merit – the absence of prejudice – and a flaw – the risk of spinning like a weathercock and always agreeing with the last person to speak. My intimate conviction is open, undecided. So now that I've taken note of what convinced me in the prosecution's closing remarks – just about everything – I remind myself to keep a lucid eye on how I might be spun round the other way.

A scare

A strange thing happened at the beginning of the third day of the prosecution's closing remarks. The fluorescent ceiling lights suddenly dimmed. They didn't go out altogether, we weren't plunged into darkness, but they dimmed, at least by half. Someone must have pressed the wrong switch. After a couple of seconds everything returned to normal, there was almost no time to get scared. Almost. But almost not scared is almost scared. The plaintiffs were scared. Those from the Bataclan were scared, remembering the blinding white light. For a moment we thought the curtain was tearing again.

Second fiddles?

The sound of hooves

'When I walk in a park in Brussels and hear the sound of hooves, I think of a horse, not a zebra. The prosecution thinks of a zebra. My client is a drug dealer. He goes to meet other drug dealers in a city, Rotterdam, which is widely reputed to be a place where it's easy to buy drugs. What does the prosecution conclude? That he went to buy weapons!' So argues Jonathan De Taye, one of Ali El Haddad Asufi's three lawyers. This is the end of the first week devoted to the defence of the accused whom the prosecution refuses to acknowledge as second fiddles on the grounds that in matters of terrorism there are no second fiddles. And as I'd anticipated, after being almost one hundred per cent convinced by the arguments of the Hennetier–Braconnay–Le Bris trio, I'm now, let's say, fifty per cent convinced by the lawyers who're demolishing them.

Clear as day

'He could not have been unaware': this phrase and its many variants lie at the heart of the charge of criminal terrorist association, which can be seen as a catch-all term, a grey area, a machine for attributing blame that works by probing souls instead of sticking to the facts. Hamza Attou was friends with Brahim Abdeslam, whose radicalisation, says the prosecution, was clear as day. Attou should have seen the danger and denounced him. Delphine Paci, one of Attou's two lawyers: 'Imagine your neighbour's an anti-vaxxer. He's been chewing your ear off about conspiracy theories. What do you do? You shrug your shoulders. One day he shoots up a vaccination centre. Should they put you in jail for not denouncing him? The Belgian police were unable to measure Brahim's dangerousness, why should a 21-year-old drug dealer be able to?' (An attractive but specious argument: the Belgian police did not see Brahim every day.) Another accusation: 'Brahim claimed to be going on holiday to Turkey. How could Attou not have known that Brahim was in fact going to Syria when he went with him to the airport? That's clearly why he was accompanying him, why else would he have gone?' Attou's response, quoted by his lawyer: 'I don't know if it's the same with you, sir, but in Molenbeek when a friend goes to buy a baguette, we go with him. Sometimes even five of us go with him.'

In whose eyes?

All of the above was clear as day, but in whose eyes? In their rebuttal of the prosecution's final statement, the defence lawyers argue that the public prosecutors are very intelligent people who, like many other very intelligent people, falsely believe that everyone else is as intelligent as they are. Instead of putting themselves in the place of guys like Ali Oulkadi, Hamza Attou or Abdellah Chouaa, who are all a bit slow on the uptake, they're surprised that Ali Oulkadi, Hamza Attou and Abdellah Chouaa have neither the keen minds nor the civic reflexes of Camille Hennetier, Nicolas Braconnay and Nicolas Le Bris. And not just the civic reflexes: the class reflexes. It's certain: the public prosecutors do not go to the bakery in groups of five. And if they go to Florence, they don't forget to visit the Uffizi Galleries. I thought back to the hearing dealing with the motives of Salah Abdeslam and his friend Ahmed Dahmani in taking their whirlwind road trip through Italy to Greece in the summer of 2015. Why drive non-stop two days there and two days back when there's so much to see on the way? Abdeslam's answer: 'No doubt you can afford more luxurious holidays, Your Honour, we can't.' And justice has always been more or less like that: the penal code was invented to prevent the poor from stealing from the rich, and the civil code to allow the rich to steal from the poor. Except that in this case – and here the prosecution has a point – the defendants are not poor. They're not rich either, granted, but they're not welfare cases, they didn't grow up in dysfunctional families, so please let's not fall prey to the accusation of 'sociological blackmail'. The prosecution seems to love that expression:

'sociological blackmail'. But just what sort of things does it cover? – asks Attou's other lawyer Delphine Boesel. Taking an interest in the defendants' social and cultural milieu: is that sociological blackmail? Admitting that everything is not in their power, that they don't carry out all of their acts after mature and informed deliberation, and that they're also the product of something bigger than they are: is that sociological blackmail? We judge not only acts but also people, and it's the role of the judiciary to put itself on the level of these people. In any case it's the role of the defence. Again and again at this extraordinary V13 trial it's been stressed just how crucial it is that this role should be respected. Not to worry: it is.

Those who should have but didn't

Even their counsel acknowledges that Muhammad Usman and Adel Haddadi should have participated in the attacks. Even the prosecution admits that they did not. Arrested on the island of Kos, they were delayed in their journey. They should have been in Paris on 13 November, they were in Slovenia. In normal cases this is what is called an airtight alibi, and leads to acquittal even if the defendant had criminal intent. In terrorism cases the defendant's intent is enough to warrant sentencing, and the two men face twenty years in prison. We're not far from *Minority Report*, Steven Spielberg's film based on a short story by Philip K. Dick, where people are arrested before they've committed the crime that a software predicts they'll commit. This is totally against the law, but in this particular case almost universally accepted. Why only in this case? There are other horrible crimes and, as Ali El Haddad Asufi's lawyer Ménya Arab-Tigrine pointed out, we're not yet preventively arresting every man who wears a cassock on charges of paedophilia. No matter: this obvious, irrefutable argument, which should close the debate – I repeat: justice cannot be preventive, people are judged according to what they have done, not what they could have done, should have done or almost did do – has become inaudible, irrelevant, with the result that a lawyer as excellent as Edward Huylebrouck, at the end of a final defence statement in all points remarkable, can say something as lame as: 'Perhaps when he arrived in Mozart's town of Salzburg, Mr Usman was struck by a sense of humanity.' Perhaps.

Life is Beautiful

Among the minor defendants, Farid Kharkhach is the odd man out. He's the middleman who supplied the cell with fake IDs. As his file doesn't show the slightest hint of radicalisation, the prosecution accuses him of colluding with jihadism out of naked greed. This greed earned him 300 euros, for which he's been sitting in prison for six years with no certainty of getting out any time soon.

Throughout the trial he's surprised everyone with his capricious moods, his sudden bursts of verbosity, his seclusiveness (he doesn't know any of the other defendants), and the incredible, almost burlesque succession of failures and fiascos that made my colleague at *L'Obs* Violette Lazard give him the nickname Bad Luck Farid. Marie Lefrancq, one of his lawyers, describes him as a loving father who didn't dare explain to his young children why he hadn't been home for six years. First he said he was ill and undergoing treatment in France. Then the children came to see him in prison, and he said he was now a prison guard. I'm not making this up. Although she wasn't present, Marie Lefrancq guarantees the authenticity of the scene: Farid Kharkhach welcomes his children in the visiting room and tells them that he's not a prisoner but a guard. I don't know how this is actually possible, but I remembered another film, *Life is Beautiful*, in which Roberto Benigni convinces his little boy that the Nazi prison where they're interned is actually a summer camp, and I thought that if Kharkhach doesn't get off too badly one could say with a fair degree of certainty that his sad story would make an incredible comedy.

Last-ditch efforts

Almost nothing to hope for

Last week was dedicated to the 'minor' defendants, who paradoxically risk a lot. Some of them hope to be acquitted, those in prison fear they may have to remain there, those who are now free are terrified they may have to go back. Suspense. The big fish Ayari, Bakkali, Krayem, Abrini and Abdeslam, meanwhile, have everything to fear and almost nothing to hope for. They know that they'll receive heavy sentences, their lawyers know it, and the closing statements resemble last-ditch efforts. The most eloquent are not necessarily the most effective, but what chance do you stand of being effective when the charges are this weighty and you're addressing not a popular jury but five professional magistrates who can see you coming a mile off and already have a more than solid grasp of all you stand to say? In that respect I liked what Mohamed Abrini's Belgian lawyer Stanislas Eskenazi said to the court: 'Your Honours, once the facts have been settled on, remove your gowns. Pass sentence as humans, not as magistrates. Only that way can this tribunal live up to its vocation as a jury court.'

The knife thrower

As the criminal stakes were low, the court was free to appreciate the talent on display. 'Well, what'd you think?' we'd ask each other during the breaks. Everyone had their favourites; I'll cite two of mine. The first is another Belgian lawyer, Isa Gultaslar, defence counsel for Sofien Ayari. Tall and gaunt with an angular face, he hardly opened his mouth during the entire trial. When his turn came to speak he created a surprise by treading new ground. Not quite a Vergès-style defence of rupture, but almost. He began by telling the story of Hamza Ali al-Khateeb, a thirteen-year-old Syrian boy who disappeared at a protest march in April 2011, at the start of the Arab Spring. Uninterested in politics, Hamza had joined his family at a rally to break the siege of the city of Daraa, where twenty-three schoolchildren had been rounded up and tortured after one of them scribbled 'It's your turn, doctor' on a wall – the doctor being Bashar al-Assad, who as we know is an ophthalmologist. Arrested by the police, Hamza was tortured to death and returned to his family with his face blackened, his body burnt, his neck broken and his genitals severed. This was Gultaslar's way of reminding us that at the heart of what is being judged at V13 lies the barbarity of the Syrian regime, and that what pushed so many young Muslims like his client towards the Islamic State is not necessarily cruelty or fanaticism, but legitimate political indignation. The cause of the attacks, he says, is not religion but war. France is militarily involved in Syria, meaning that it is at war. Hence the crimes committed in Paris by the Islamic State fighters should fall not under national anti-terrorist law but under the international law of armed conflict. And so they should be reclassified as war crimes. A stir. Is there any chance, eight days before the verdict is to be handed down, of the entire trial being reclassified? Would it improve Sofien Ayari's already dismal prospects? I don't think so; nevertheless the court was witness to an impressive lesson in law, geopolitics and oration. During the break stories circulated about Gultaslar, whom very few had known much about before he spoke. He was part of a Belgian support committee for Osama Atar before the latter became the head of the Islamic State's external operations wing, some said. This is true, and reinforces Gultaslar's Vergès side. And before being a lawyer he was a knife thrower at amusement parks. It was Georges Salines who told me that, and I only realised that he was pulling my leg when I summoned my courage and asked Gultaslar if it was true. He smiled politely and said that no, it wasn't, and what's more he'd never been a bear tamer in Bhutan and was not Keyser Söze either. Nevertheless he is someone who invites such questions, and when he entered the brasserie Les Deux Palais after the hearing he was given a round of applause.

Soaring

As I didn't go there that day I don't know if Orly Rezlan was applauded at Les Deux Palais, but she had every reason to be. She's one of Mohamed Bakkali's lawyers, and I have to admit that I found her dislikeable. Her voice was unpleasant and her tone crabby: she didn't try to seduce us in her final statement any more than she had over the course of the hearings. But as she progressed, her austere manner, her power of conviction and her monotonous, throbbing anger rose from level to level without her raising her voice, until they attained a hypnotic quality that Soren Seelow, terrorism specialist at *Le Monde*, fittingly described as 'soaring'. Orly Rezlan's plea soared. Unrelentingly. And like Gultaslar's it brought something new, something we hadn't heard before, and which, although it is of course not an excuse, could be seen as the start of an explanation. Only whereas Gultaslar stressed political indignation, Rezlan accentuated the pangs of conscience that go with any sustained religious practice. Am I a good Muslim? Have I done enough to support my brothers in need? When others suffer and fight, is it not shameful to hide away in a life of comfort? These questions are tough in themselves, but Rezlan went further. Instead of quoting Camus as has been done to the point of nausea, she made a striking reference to Sebastian Haffner's *Defying Hitler: A Memoir**, one of the great books

---

* Sebastian Haffner, *Defying Hitler: A Memoir*, Weidenfeld & Nicolson, 2012.

on the rise of Nazism – read it, give it to others to read. Haffner was a young lawyer – well, well – who described and tried to understand how so many young people his age who were neither psychopaths nor even extremists allowed themselves to be caught up in the hate machine. For many, he concluded, the motivation was camaraderie, pure and simple. You share an ideal, you're united in indignation: adhering to the values of the group shows that you're a good guy. It's walking on thin ice to argue that you can participate in attacks or genocide because you're a good person at heart. But because you're a good comrade? That adds up.

A whole life order

Then the time came for Abdeslam's two young lawyers, Martin Vettes and Olivia Ronen, to speak. Full house. They were good, very good, and Ronen, in her last quarter of an hour, was what can only be called inspired. They pleaded their case, at length, valiantly, but their real fight, the one that has a chance of succeeding, is against the whole life order, the real, 'incompressible' life sentence demanded by the prosecution. This maximum maximum sentence has been handed down four times since 1994, each time for sadists and extreme perverts like the serial killer Michel Fourniret, who pose an extreme threat to society. Abdeslam deserves a heavy sentence, nobody denies that, but he is not Fourniret. He's not even Abdelhamid Abaaoud, or Osama Atar. Giving him this horrendous sentence would mean running roughshod over the proportionality of sentences just to set an example – in which case, Ronen concluded, 'if you agree with the prosecution, terrorism will have won'.

Two things I find a shame

I didn't like that ending. It's the role of the defence to rebut the prosecution. Ronen does so vehemently, fine. But from the beginning to the end of her closing arguments she was more than scathing, she was insulting. And I found that a shame. One could criticise the Hennetier–Braconnay–Le Bris trio for being far too harsh in their sentencing demands. I too hope that their call for a 'real', i.e. a whole, life sentence will not be heeded. But one cannot say they were either mediocre or demagogic, let alone 'execrable', as Ronen maintained. They really weren't. On the contrary, one of V13's true strengths was the impeccable standard of the prosecution. And while we're on the subject of things I find a shame, here's another. Judge Périès's last words were to warn those present that the verdict, scheduled for 5 p.m. on Wednesday 29 July, would probably not be delivered until late in the evening. 'I am well aware,' he added, 'that this wait will be trying for the plaintiffs and will not suit the needs of the press, but we have no choice.' Once again: fine. What I find a shame, though, is that he forgot to mention that it would no doubt also be trying for the defendants.

The end

In the Auction Room

The verdict is scheduled for 5 p.m., we're pretty sure it will be handed down later, some think very late at night. Even more people than on the first day, even more gendarmes, even more fever in the air. We want to stay close to the action, we pace back and forth, chocolate bars and rumours circulate. As on the first day, there's only one seat per media outlet in the courtroom proper, this time the one for *L'Obs* goes to Mathieu. Violette and I secure places in the Salle des Criées, or Auction Room, where monitors display the proceedings. Violette perches on the corner of a bench, I crouch on a step at the back. In former days candlelit auctions were held in this august courtroom, today it's packed with two hundred journalists from all over the world, most of whom we're seeing for the first time. The court makes its entrance at 8.30 p.m., we'd feared it would be even later. The full judgement is 120 pages long, the presiding judge announces, it'll be available during the night, for now he'll only read a summary. 'No objections?' He laughs at his joke, you can sense he's on edge, everyone is. He reads. Except in the case of the defendant Farid

Kharkhach, the court answers yes to all of the questions raised by the prosecution. With the exception of Farid Kharkhach, all of the defendants are found guilty on all counts. Kharkhach is the moody dude who made the fake IDs, plainly not knowing for whom or what, and who passes himself off as a guard when his children come to see him in prison. We're happy for Kharkhach, but if he's the only one to come off lightly that means that for all the others their number is up. This is also what the three minor defendants, Chouaa, Attou and Oulkadi, understand. Throughout the trial they've appeared free on their folding seats in front of the box, now they plunge their heads in their hands and sob. At their feet are zipped plastic shopping bags containing their belongings in case they're sent straight to prison. And even if this is not yet certain because their full sentence must still be handed down, it seems likely. I remember Chouaa's final words the day before last: 'I'm so afraid you'll make a mistake.' These are the two great uncertainties about the verdict: the fate of the minor defendants – will they go free? – and that of the main defendant Abdeslam – will he get the notorious, and for many shocking, whole life order demanded by the prosecution? When Judge Périès announces his sentence it's not entirely clear either, because after saying 'life sentence', which surprises no one, he adds that none of the measures provided for in Article 132-23 of the Penal Code can be applied. We suspect that this is not good news for Abdeslam, he himself seems disconcerted and shoots a questioning look over at his lawyers who appear troubled, but as Périès did not in fact say the word 'incompressible' – meaning a whole life order – everyone on the benches starts asking: 'What did he say? What's in Article 132-23?' Journalists from all over the world have just half an hour to file, shoot or tweet their reports: the pressure's on. Judge Périès continues reading. This usually unflappable man stumbles over his words and makes slips of the tongue, the most spectacular being when he calls Mohammed Amri Mohammed Henry – which for a judge his age is not at all anodyne when you recall that the child killer who was snatched from the guillotine immediately prior to the abolition of the death penalty was named Patrick Henry. And it's right after that, Mohammed Henry, that the image freezes on the screen. The presiding judge goes immobile with a stunned look on his face, the sound is gone, the display is interrupted. Glitch.

The general stutters

Two-thirds of the way through the verdict, in the middle of the sentencing, at the most dramatic moment of the trial, a glitch. Unbelievable. We're left hanging, waiting for the transmission to resume. It doesn't. We're at a loss. Some people stay rooted to the spot, others go out into the hall. I go out. We gather in front of the white box where the sentencing continues. Of course we can't go in, it's full to bursting. But, we stammer, there'll be a recess? Until it's fixed? There'll be no recess, says Julien Quéré, of whom I'll speak shortly. The sentencing goes on inside, general consternation outside. Which I share, until I remember this story. In 1849, at the age of twenty-eight, Dostoevsky was arrested for engaging in subversive activities and sentenced to death. Together with the other members of his revolutionary group he was taken to the place of his execution. They were hooded and tied to posts while the firing squad loaded their rifles. Just before the order was given to fire, an envoy of the Tsar arrived and read a message announcing their pardon. A relative pardon: Dostoevsky served four years in a prison camp in Siberia, from where he'll return as Dostoevsky, the man who will later describe in *Demons* the hotbed of distraught minds that is a terrorist cell. The sublime detail, which his biographers never tire of telling, is that, either by chance or by pure sadism, the envoy charged with reading the letter of pardon was a *stuttering general*. I can imagine what happened in the courtroom right after the display in the Auction Room was interrupted. The presiding judge was no doubt alerted and had to decide immediately: should the hearing be suspended until the glitch was fixed on the grounds that you can't do that to the two hundred journalists who'd come in from all over the world, or, since things were already under way, should they not be stopped on the grounds that you can't do that to the defendants? In the last chapter I said I found it a shame that Judge Périès had shown concern for everyone but the defendants regarding the length of the deliberation. Today he made up for that spectacularly by saying: the show must go on. He refused to be the stuttering general.

(Now that I've come this far: it's said that a psychoanalysis is played out entirely in the first session, and the same is true of a first court hearing. When asked about his profession, Abdeslam answers: 'Islamic State fighter.' Judge Périès looks at his notes and says: 'It says here: temporary worker.' This line has become legendary and could not have been premeditated, it came without any *added* humour or sarcasm. And it established Périès's authority for the length of the trial. From the first hearing to the one hundred and forty-ninth: hats off to him.)

At the top of the steps

We're standing at the top of the steps of the Palais de Justice, and Marie Dosé is griping up a storm. Marie Dosé defended Ali Oulkadi together with Judith Lévy, and they both have reason to be happy because Oulkadi and the other two minor defendants will go free after all. But it takes more than that to satisfy Marie Dosé, who's a passionate, stubborn, irascible lawyer – I adore her. This verdict is nonsense, she says. From a legal point of view. They'd demanded Oulkadi's acquittal. He's found guilty of everything: criminal terrorist association, harbouring terrorist criminals, extremely serious things, and what does he get? Two years in prison that he's already served, the same as you'd get in a summary trial for snatching a bag. And what does it mean? That the court knows full well it doesn't have anything terrible to accuse him of. But instead of acquitting him or giving him two years for harbouring a criminal, which would correspond to the truth, they want to set as a precedent that nothing can escape the verdict of criminal terrorist association – which was already a bullshit offence and is now becoming a legal rubbish dump. The whole point of the judgement, they explain (I like it when Marie Dosé and Judith Lévy explain things, they often did it during the trial), is to forestall an appeal. Anything but an appeal. For now they're not considering appealing the decision. It's completely absurd, Oulkadi will be stamped a terrorist for the rest of his life, but he'll go free, that's the main thing. The same goes for Chouaa and Attou. In general, the court gave everyone *a little less* than what the prosecution demanded – the subtext being: consider yourselves lucky, and if you do appeal you can be sure you'll get more – so as to bring the full weight of the law down on Salah Abdeslam, the absolute, definitive, terminal terrorist who will stay in jail until his dying day, and that way everyone will be happy. Well, everyone: the public, who'll be sent the message that there is no pity in matters of terrorism. But certainly not everyone I know at the trial, including the plaintiffs, most of whom feel uncomfortable with this sentence which has only been handed down four times in a quarter of a century. If they feel that way it's for two reasons, one having to do with common sense, the other with the law. Common sense: if the nine killers who made up the commando weren't dead but here in the box, they would have received – and deserved – this 'incompressible' whole life order. And Abdeslam in that case? What would he, the feckless second fiddle, have got? Not the same punishment, that's for dead sure. But we don't have the real criminals on hand, so he's being made to pay for them. And legal: the sentence is based on a twisted legal construction. Legally speaking, even if you add up everything Abdeslam is guilty of, it doesn't allow you to sentence him to the absolute, incompressible maximum. By any measure, it doesn't tally. What would help is if he'd shot at the police at the Bataclan. But not only did he not shoot at anyone, he wasn't at the Bataclan. No problem, the prosecution says, what we'll do is consider all the scenes of the attack a single scene of attack. *Not shooting* in a café in the 18th arrondissement is equivalent to *shooting* in a concert hall in the 11th. That is what's termed the 'interchangeability' of theatres, the territorial transposition of the adage 'if it's not you, it's your brother', and the motor behind the sentence of criminal terrorist association. Nevertheless for all the esteem I have for the prosecution, it leaves me baffled. I'm baffled by it, many of my fellows at the trial are baffled by it. But tonight we cannot honestly say that our bafflement will get the better of us. We're not going to launch the hashtag *#iamsalah* tonight. Fine, the merits of the verdict can be debated, but however you look at it it's not scandalous, and half an hour after it was handed down we've moved on. We're at the top of these steps where we've lingered so often, talking, smoking, crying during the recesses. Thirty riot vans are parked on the boulevard down below. In a few hours they'll leave, and after being cordoned off for almost a year the Île de la Cité will once again be open to traffic. I don't know how many times friends have said to me over the last months: I'm sick of your trial and its roadblocks. *My* trial, yes. Tonight all of us, even those like me who were only here as observers, realise that it was *our* trial. And it's over.

We walk down the steps

I walk down the steps with Aurélie, whose partner Mathieu was killed at the Bataclan. I haven't mentioned her in these columns, that's often how it is with ephemeral communities: there are people you only make friends with at the end. She tells me: on 14 November 2015 her sister turned off the television and said: as of now you don't watch anything, you don't listen to anything, you don't stew over all of this, you concentrate on your life. Aurélie's beautiful book *Nos 14 novembre** (Our fourteenths of November) talks about Mathieu, their children, mourning, intimacy, life, but not *that*. She refuses to let it get to her. There's no question of her going to the trial,

* Aurélie Silvestre, *Nos 14 novembre*, Lattès, 2016.

let alone testifying. On 8 September 2021, a friend from the Bataclan insists that she come along: it's a historic moment, she should at least come and check it out. She drags her feet but goes, determined to stop before the first police checkpoint. However, when they get there she's tempted to go in, which is of course impossible because she's got nothing, no accreditation, no badge, not even any ID. At the checkpoint a thin, nervous guy appears, they explain the problem, he tells the gendarmes to let her in, and the next day they make her a badge. The thin, nervous guy is Julien Quéré, he's the magistrate responsible for organising the entire trial, and it's important to put his name down in black and white because almost everyone here has a story like this to tell, one where Julien Quéré appears and resolves the most inextricable situations with tact and efficiency bordering on the supernatural. He was in charge of organisation, all of his subordinates were just like him, and I believe that no one, none of the plaintiffs and in general none of those who attended the trial in any capacity, felt treated negligently in any way. Pascale Robert-Diard from *Le Monde*, the out-and-out heroine of all the court reporters, wrote an article that ruffled quite a few feathers, saying that it was all very well to see to the victims' needs, but that things were being taken to extremes and there was no need to cocoon them like that. Although normally I'm the first to agree with such a position, the fact is that over the course of the trial this cocoon proved precious, and everyone was happy to receive such treatment. Everyone was grateful. Everyone says: it's amazing *how well* everything went. Aurélie enters the courtroom and takes stock of this big white box. The glass box with the accused is far away on the left. She doesn't want to see them, but around her she discovers survivors, mourners, fellow humans whose lives have been cleaved in two. A few days later the presiding judge calls the ghostly roll: the names of the 130 dead resound in an all-embracing silence and she feels in her body, like a wave, the collective dimension of what is going on there in the room, something larger than herself, and she understands that she's going to take part. She comes from time to time at first, then more and more often. At first she sits at the back, then she comes closer. At first she doesn't look to the left, at the box, then she starts looking, at this dangerous, irradiated area. A clear line separates the victims who come to take the stand: there are those who turn to the left at one point to look at the accused, address them, and those who would not do so for anything in the world. Then comes the day when Aurélie testifies, leaving the courtroom deeply shaken. The newspapers that cover it headline: 'I've become an athlete of mourning'. She starts going to Les Deux Palais. She gets to know the others. The absolute low point of V13 comes at the start of the winter with the run of Belgian investigators. Everyone is bored stiff and even that doesn't discourage her. For Georges Salines, who's not afraid to speak his mind, it's an addiction. And everyone I talk to says the same thing. They got caught up in it, it was fascinating even when it was boring, once you were on there was no getting off. My personal experience carries less weight, but I too said to myself at the start: we'll see. In principle I'll attend the whole trial, but if I've had enough after three months I'll tell my friends at *L'Obs* that I'm throwing in the towel. We'll all be a little disappointed but it won't be a huge deal. Never, not once, did I so much as think of it. Not once did I want to say goodbye to the white box. I knew, we knew, that what we were experiencing was anything but the grand historical event, the vain, colossal judicial spectacle that we all had good reason to fear at the beginning. No: this was something else: a unique experience of horror, pity, proximity and presence. It was only very late in the day that I realised that the white box resembles a modern church, and that something sacred had been taking place there. Aurélie: 'We were given a place, and time, all the time we needed, to do something with the pain. Transform it, metabolise it. And it worked. It happened. We departed, we made this long, long crossing, and now the ship is coming into port. It's time to disembark.'

We go for a drink.

At Les Deux Palais

Sorry if this sounds frivolous, it's not. That evening was the most extraordinary one I have ever spent – and probably will ever spend – in my entire life. Anyone who was there will tell you the same thing. In small groups, we descended the courthouse steps and flocked across the street to Les Deux Palais, that magical Balzacian brasserie where for several generations magistrates, lawyers, journalists and litigants have gathered at all hours in a rustle of black robes and often in the wake of tragedy, next to couples who've just divorced and are having an awkward, sad coffee together before going off to their new lives. As the police checkpoint will still be in place for the next couple of hours you still have to show your badge to access this little parcel of the Île de la Cité, which for that reason is as good as reserved for us. We who will go our separate ways tonight, and who've spent so many hours on these red booth seats at these varnished wooden tables, are the only ones in the brasserie. We're all there, and a good third of those present are plaintiffs, enough so that the ones who did not suffer a loss, those who like me are on the other side of the fence, can tell themselves that this evening's strange jubilation is not indecent. Or is it? Is it indecent that Hamza, Abdellah and Ali, who've got off by the skin of their teeth but nevertheless played their part in the service of death are also here, being congratulated and kissed and posing for selfies with amazed looks on their faces, and not believing their luck? The question is legitimate, the answers vary. A young woman who was severely handicapped because she had the bad idea of celebrating her birthday at La Belle Équipe left with her partner because they found the show obscene. 'I got more kisses tonight than at my wedding,' says Ali Oulkadi. His two pals are banned from France for ten years, but we'll just say those ten years start tomorrow, and tonight even the public prosecutors watch them with fondness as they warm to their growing fan club. So distant, almost intimidating during the hearings, never milling around with the others during the breaks, the public prosecutors now look more like friends you'd meet up with for drinks or a weekend hike – Nicolas Braconnay's hobby, so now we can't imagine him wearing anything but a fleece jacket. Camille Hennetier is wearing a summer dress, and Olivia Ronen, who defended Abdeslam with Martin Vettes and who looks so young, like a schoolgirl, comes over and says to me: 'I pissed you off, didn't I? I don't know how many times you wrote that I pissed you off.' I reply, sincerely – tonight everyone is sincere – 'Sure, you pissed me off, with your aggressiveness and your Salah here, Salah there, but I admired you. You and Martin fought like lions. I think the sentencing had been decided in advance. There was nothing you could do to change that. And at the end of your plea you walked on water, Olivia, it was beautiful.'

The flashes

We're there, we're together, we comment on the verdict, we hug, and when we promise not to lose touch I know in many cases it will be true. What we've been through was too strong, incommunicable, no one will understand who wasn't there. With the exception of those who spend the whole evening with the same gang at the same table, many of us, including myself, move from group to group and cross paths again and again. I must have bumped into Yann Revol, with whom Nadia and I explored the conspiracy bush, about ten times that night, and one of those times I remembered a bit from his testimony last autumn. When the bullets hit him he felt deeply isolated. Everything went dark. His mind fell into a calm, numbed reverie, from which he was awoken by his girlfriend Gaëlle's screams. He realised that she might die, that this was real. The three of them –Yann's brother was with them – crawled towards the kitchen of Le Petit Cambodge where a phone on the wall kept ringing and ringing, and he started to answer the calls. First it was someone who wanted to order a bobun to go, whom he told that that wouldn't be possible for the moment, and then other panic-stricken people who wanted to know what was going on, and in a stupor he kept repeating this strange phrase: everything's fine, we've been shot at but everything's fine. The wounded were moaning, the rescue workers were carrying away the bodies, and Yann, who's a photographer, had a series of flashes: seeing all of these dead, wounded and living people he didn't know, he saw them individually, each in their own particular, infinite pain, while the story of each one, the pain of each one, the soul of each one burst in slow motion like bubbles of silence and light before his eyes.

'Yes,' says Yann when I remind him of that moment that struck me so strongly, 'and you know what? They came back during the trial. Those flashes came back, and once again I had the physical sensation that the others were around me and that I had access to each one. My dream at the start was to know every detail about what happened where I was. Then my perimeter expanded. I've remained someone from Le Petit Cambodge, but little by little I got to know the people from the other terraces, then those from the Bataclan and the Stade de France, and even from the Rue du Corbillon, and I'd like to know everything about them as well.' This is how Yann ended his testimony: 'I thank you for this trial. I thank you for going into detail.' It's true, we went into detail, and I remember something else I thought last autumn, something that was a kind of flash for me. I thought that the ambition behind the V13 trial was crazy, colossal, over the top: seeking to unfold, over a period of nine months, from every angle, from the point of view of everyone involved and going as far back as possible, what led up to those few hours of horror. We tried to read the whole book. Yann and I kept working the room, on our own but sure we'd run into each other again before the end of the evening. 'You're not leaving yet?' 'No, I'll be sticking around for a while.' At V13 if you wanted to see someone you didn't have to make an appointment, you just said see you tomorrow. I'm sad when I think of all these people I'm not going to see tomorrow.

'It was good'

The bar is crowded, the orders are no longer being placed by the glass but by the bottle. The plaintiffs' lawyers send champagne over to the counsel for the defence. I haven't had a drop of alcohol in four years but tonight I'm drunk, we all are. Propped up against the counter, I lean over to hear what a journalist friend is saying: 'Are you going to do Nice?' A recurring question among the legal journalists: the trial of the truck attack that took place on the Promenade des Anglais on 14 July 2016 will open in September, in the same white courtroom. No, I say, definitely not: if it's not your job, spending the better part of one year attending a terrorism trial is enough for a lifetime. 'You're right, it'll be horrible. The facts are even more horrendous – the families, the children crushed in their prams . . . and as far as the plaintiffs go, it's not exactly the same profile as at the terraces or the Bataclan. It'll be a far cry from "you will not have my hate". Still, it'll take place over there, in the white box . . . You don't feel a smidgen of nostalgia? You won't be tempted to come over once or twice? Maybe ask for a visitor's badge?' We laugh, but he's right: once you've seen what goes down in the white box, how can you not be tempted to go back when you get the chance? I elbow my way over to the terrace where two drunk young women are flirting with the public prosecutors' impassive bodyguards. A guy I don't recognise – he couldn't have come that often – says to me: 'Kind of odd, isn't it, that it all ends on a terrace?' I nod, yes, it's kind of odd. 'The terraces have won!' he bawls. I move off and bump into Aurélie, who's taking a bottle and glasses to her table. I say what we all say: 'So it's over . . .' 'Yes,' she says, 'it's over . . .' A moment goes by, then: 'It was good. Now I can go home.'

Allahu akbar

In 2018, Nadia returned to Cairo, her home town. The last time she'd been there was in 2014, with Lamia. They'd spent a quiet moment in Al-Azhar Park, near the mosque of the same name known around the world as the heart of Sunni Islam. The sun was setting, the calls to prayer rose from the huge, swarming city, the city of cities they both loved. They listened to the cries of *Allahu Akbar* in the golden sky. They felt at peace. Four years later, Nadia sat alone, for a long time, in the place where they'd sat together for a long time. She listened to the cries of *Allahu Akbar* rising from the huge, swarming city and their echo in the golden sky. A policeman came up to tell her that the park was closing. She was the only one left, it was time to go. Nadia wanted to stay a little longer. The policeman insisted, but instead of obeying, she started to tell him, in Arabic, what had happened. The words came to her naturally, calmly, and as she spoke she understood that it was essential, that it was the most important thing she could do, to tell this story in Arabic to an unknown Egyptian policeman. The policeman understood this too. At the end of the story, he said to Nadia: your daughter and the others are *shaheed*, martyrs, and to hear from the mouth of this

Egyptian policeman that they were the martyrs, and not the killers who attributed this dignity to themselves from the depths of their crass, manipulated ignorance, it was as if the world was falling back into place.

Acknowledgements

These columns appeared in *L'Obs*, and were reprinted in *La Repubblica* in Italy, *El País* in Spain, *Le Temps* in Switzerland. I've reworked them a bit. Above all I've included passages that didn't make their way into the roughly 1,500 words I submitted to *L'Obs* each week. That explains why the book is a third longer than what appeared in the magazine.

I'd like to thank Cécile Prieur, Executive Editor at *L'Obs*, for accepting this collaboration, and Grégoire Leménager for being the ideal editor. In the afterword he generously contributes to this book he writes that I'm the ideal freelancer: be that as it may, we got on ideally. Thanks also to Violette Lazard and Mathieu Delahousse, my colleagues at *L'Obs*, for saving me from writing a good deal of nonsense.

A trial spanning almost a year is also a process of companionship and mentoring. All those who attend regularly build up an informal circle of contacts comprising journalists, plaintiffs and lawyers on both sides, with whom they discuss the case during the recesses and sometimes go for a drink afterwards. Here are some of those I would like to thank for having accompanied me along the way: Helena Christidis, Jean-Marc Delas, Arthur Dénouveaux, David De Pas, Marie Dosé, Stéphane

Durand-Souffland, Pascale Égré, David Fritz Goeppinger, Camille Gardesse, Frédérique Giffard, Negar Haeri, Camille Hennetier, Judith Lévy, Delphine Meillet, Xavier Nogueras, Vincent Nouzille, Charlotte Piret, Julien Quéré, Hélène Quiniou, Jean Reinhart, Yann Revol, Pascale Robert-Diard, Georges Salines, Henri Seckel, Soren Seelow, Aurélie Silvestre, Mathieu Suc, Isabelle Sulpicy, Sylvie Topaloff.

Nadia Mondeguer.

Postscript

A journalist
by Grégoire Leménager

The columns collected here do not come from nowhere. They have a history, a prehistory even, which perhaps needs shedding light on to understand a journalist like Emmanuel Carrère. He's someone who knows the ropes. To go back only as far as 1996, in *Le Nouvel Observateur* alone he published two articles on the 'Romand affair' which would serve as a template for his book *The Adversary*. Then in March 2012, he published, also for *Le Nouvel Observateur*, a major report on Russia which reads like a probing postscript to his *Limonov*. In 2016 these three articles joined many others to make up a fascinating book whose title sums up a quarter of a century in and around journalism: *97,196 Words*.

So there was every reason to be delighted, at the end of autumn 2020 shortly after the release of his latest book *Yoga* – which seemed to have left him somewhat out of sorts – that Emmanuel Carrère wrote a few lines to Jérôme Garcin, head of the cultural section at *L'Obs*:

Dear Jérôme,

I hope that you're doing as well as can be expected under the circumstances – that is that you and your family are in good health.

Just a note to say that I would not be at all averse to doing some reporting at the moment. The first time I told you that was in 1990, and, you'll remember, it resulted in a series of legal columns for L'Événement du jeudi. *Later I followed the Romand trial for you. So the two of us go way back. You know my work, you know the kind of stuff I'm comfortable with: less opinion pieces than fieldwork, maybe a criminal case, something on Nagorno-Karabakh. Do you think you could keep that in the back of your mind? Don't hesitate to spread the word to the other departments at* L'Obs, *maybe the society or foreign desk?*

Yours amicably,
Emmanuel

Jérôme Garcin spread the word. Together with the new editor at *L'Obs*, Cécile Prieur, and her other deputy Clément Lacombe, we met with Carrère and tossed around a couple of ideas. Things quickly took shape. He resolved to lock himself up for ten days in the Department of Child and Adolescent Psychiatry of the Pitié-Salpêtrière Hospital, emerging for Christmas with 'The Children of Pity', a moving ten-page account of a harsh and little-known reality which we were proud to publish in January 2021.

*

Emmanuel Carrère also seemed happy with his report on these adolescents, whose lives had been turned upside down during the Covid epidemic. So we decided to pitch another idea at him: to cover the entire, historic trial of the terrible attacks of 13 November 2015, which was due to get under way in September. Of course, between Violette Lazard, Mathieu Delahousse and Vincent Monnier, the magazine had no shortage of excellent reporters for the V13 trial. But to cover this huge event, which would be the subject of an equally huge media hype, from a slightly different perspective, everything in Carrère's CV indicated that he would be a good addition to our team. In *The Adversary* he had told the story of an unusual murderer who had himself practised a sort of *taqîya*, or dissimulation, by hiding a good part of his existence from his family. In *Other Lives But Mine* he had highlighted the pain of mourning. In *The Kingdom* he'd investigated the roots of religious radicalisation. And he'd just adapted Florence Aubenas's *The Night Cleaner* – which on reflection also tells a story of *taqîya* – for the cinema.

The more we kicked around the idea of his covering this monster trial, the more we thought we should at least run it by him, just in case it appealed to him. (I specify 'just in case' because, to be honest, we weren't at all sure that someone like Carrère who, when he's not busy shooting a film, devotes a large part of his time to writing books or getting out and about, could agree to spending months on end uncomfortably seated in a maximum-security courtroom listening to hearings that are as gruelling as they are endless.) The problem was that in order to put our proposal to him we would have to hear from him. A few friendly messages written in such a way that it was clear we had something to ask him went unanswered. Emmanuel Carrère had politely disappeared off the radar.

He resurfaced on 11 May 2021 with a very direct and passably enigmatic text message which, I now realise, suits him to a T: *Grégoire, I'd like a word with you. A coffee between neighbours? Emmanuel.* We weren't exactly neighbours, but whatever. I proposed a couple of dates, he fired back: *Tomorrow afternoon is fine. Whenever suits you. You'll come over to my place?* His place, I quickly understood when I entered, was not going to be his for much longer. It was completely empty, furnished exclusively with piles of boxes which were to be moved out the following weekend. I was in the middle of a move myself – that gave us something to talk about for about four minutes. He couldn't have waited much longer than that to get to the point: he had his mind set on following the 13 November trial, he saw it as the subject of his next book, and before working on the book proper he wanted to tell the story in the form of weekly columns in a newspaper or magazine. As he sketched it out, his project didn't go much further than that. He was like a pianist preparing for a huge concert by imposing on himself a disciplined framework for practising, independent of his moods. For now he knew exactly what he wanted: to go to court, every day, the way other people go to work. After half an hour I was out the door.

Did Emmanuel Carrère get his idea for the 13 November trial from Yannick Haenel's coverage of the trial dealing with the January 2015 *Charlie Hebdo* attack? In any case, setting up a clear agenda with regular reports struck him as essential: his key demand was that a fixed space in the magazine should be set aside for his columns, always the same length, no matter how interesting or uninteresting the debates might be or whatever else was going on in the news. We quickly agreed on the length: 1,400 words, to be submitted every Monday morning at the latest. These 1,400 words sometimes swelled to 1,450, even 1,500 words*, which our layout artists always magically fitted into the two-page spread reserved for them, but I was never left waiting. Working with Emmanuel Carrère amounts to working with the perfect journalist, one who makes a point of delivering perfect copy every week, perfectly on time, without the slightest syntax error or problem with readability. A journalist who, on top of everything else, answers immediately when we run by him an idea for a headline or a minor change. (These qualities may seem to go without saying, but no doubt every editor in the world wishes at one point or other that they were more common in the profession.)

And that's how it came to pass that every day, with his colleagues from *L'Obs*, his marathon runner's stamina and his thick red notebook in which he suddenly

---

* To give an idea, this postscript is itself 1,453 words long.

scribbled things down during the hearings, this journalist confined himself for ten months to the large white
wooden box in the heart of Paris with an orange cord
around his neck, sitting uncomfortably on the hard
wooden benches. That's how it happened that every
week, from 2 September 2021 to 7 July 2022, he detailed
for *L'Obs*'s readers the dreadful, bloody, teary tale of
that cursed 13 November 2015. And that's how, for
almost a year, each of my weekends ended with a ritual
that I miss already: reading, editing and experiencing the
roughly 1,400 words sent to me by Emmanuel Carrère.

Grégoire Leménager is deputy editor of L'Obs.

A NOTE ABOUT THE AUTHOR

Emmanuel Carrère, born in Paris in 1957, is a novelist, journalist, screenwriter, and film producer. He is the award-winning, internationally renowned author of *Yoga*, *97,196 Words*, *The Kingdom*, *Limonov*, *The Mustache*, *Class Trip*, *The Adversary* (a *New York Times* Notable Book), *My Life as a Russian Novel*, and *Lives Other Than My Own*, which was awarded the Globe de Cristal for Best Novel in 2010. For *Limonov*, Carrère received the Prix Renaudot and the Prix des Prix in 2011 and the Europese Literatuurprijs in 2013.

A NOTE ABOUT THE TRANSLATOR

John Lambert has translated *Monsieur*, *Reticence*, and *Self-Portrait Abroad*, by Jean-Philippe Toussaint, as well as Emmanuel Carrère's *Yoga*, *97,196 Words*, *The Kingdom*, and *Limonov*.